VOICES
OF THE
ARMORY

A CHRONICLE OF THE TRANSFORMATION OF A
19TH CENTURY ICON INTO A 21ST CENTURY THEATER

Narrative by Chris Coleman *Artistic Director, Portland Center Stage*
Photography by Kurt Goetzinger and Christopher Smith

CONTRIBUTORS: Sam Adams; Susan Anderson; Elaine Aye and Alan Scott; Alan Beard; Victoria Blake; Jack Bogan with Jim Hultquist, Heather McAvoy and Rose Steele; Zachary Boyers; Pat Conrad; Tobin Cooley; Stuart Cowan; Sherri Diteman; Bob Gerding; Randy Gragg; The Felt Hat; Mead Hunter; Brad Johnson; Jamey Hampton; Mel Katz; Nancy Keystone and Peter Maradudin; Bart King; Bob Kingston; Brian Libby; Norris Lozano; Don Mazziotti; Julie Metcalf Kinney; Scott Murase; Michael J. Novogradac; J. Greg Ness; Chet Orloff; Blake Patsy; Colin Rowan; Edwin Schlossberg; Bob Schroeder; Todd Stern; Herbert F. Stevens; Carl Talton; John Terry; John Tess; Julie Vigeland; Wieden + Kennedy 12

Managing Editor: Christopher Smith

PUBLISHED BY FRIENDS OF THE ARMORY
AND PORTLAND FAMILY OF FUNDS HOLDINGS, INC.

TABLE OF CONTENTS

PHOTOGRAPHY

Kurt Goetzinger and Christopher Smith with additional photography by Sherri Diteman

PRESERVING AN ICON THE PORTLAND WAY:

A Play in Six Acts with a Cast of Thousands *by Norris Lozano*

In Portland, Oregon, on the corner of NW Davis and 10th Avenues stands a castle-like building that has stood for over a century. On the northwest corner of that building is a sandstone plaque. "Annex 1891," it says, reminding us this is the Annex to the original First Regiment Armory, built four years earlier. Underneath there appears to be a filigree of some sort in a rectangular field.

A closer inspection reveals that the filigree is actually hand-chiseled script that says, McCaw & Martin, Architects.

I welcome you to *Voices of the Armory* in this way because, like all historic buildings, this one is full of stories. Most of these might have been lost to history had our Armory not been preserved. The original Armory, which stood next door and was felled in 1968, is evidence of this possibility.

Thankfully, after nearly four years of planning and construction, this iconic building, now called The Gerding Theater at the Armory is open to the public, reimagined and renovated on four pillars: history, theater, sustainability and community.

Why, you might ask, would so much be asked of one building?

The answer is: Because honoring the past, celebrating the humanity, sustaining the natural environment, and giving back to the community are among the highest and best values we share in Portland, and the Armory has the broad shoulders to carry them all. Because, from the highest levels of politics, finance, architecture and design, to the artisans who painstakingly preserved the building's original stone, brick, even window frames, the many project partners had the will to deliver not only a financially successful project — the bottom line — but one that delivers maximum social and environmental benefits as well.

This triple bottom line is the core of our mission at Portland Family of Funds, and it's shared by many of our partners. As you'll read in these pages, the hard work of hundreds of people across the country has contributed to the success of this project. But the momentum was built and sustained for these four years by the vision and courage of five people whom I'd like to acknowledge here.

Ed Jensen, former vice chairman and chief operating officer of US Bancorp when it was headquartered in Portland, went on to become president and chief executive officer of Visa International. Upon "retiring" he came home to Portland with a goal in mind: to bring new financial resources to our city to help propel it into the 21st century. Ed was the founding executive chair of Portland Family of Funds (PFF) whose mission is to create opportunities for profitable investments that enhance social and environmental yields. Ed brought together a board consisting of Ralph Shaw, Marty Brantley, Mike Henderson, Molly Bordonaro and Carl Talton. As of October 2006, PFF has financed projects including the Armory which are anticipated to encourage the creation of more than 5,500 construction and permanent jobs, bring approximately $260.5 million in new fiscal resources to Portland, and an estimated $1.7 billion in total economic impacts over the next decade.

The Portland Development Commission (PDC) is internationally respected as an urban development agency that "gets it" when it comes to the intelligent design of a city. In 2000, Don Mazziotti was brought back to Portland to head the organization. With the economy showing signs of weakening, Don recognized that the PDC would need new resources to continue to execute its mission. One of these resources was New Markets Tax Credits (NMTC), a new federal program that will ultimately provide $15 billion in

Preserving an Icon *continued*

tax credits allocation to attract private investment into challenged communities. The Armory was one of the first NMTC deals to close, and just two years later, there are a dozen significant NMTC projects in Portland, including an elementary school, a medical office, a drug rehabilitation facility, several historic preservations, even a new loan fund for small businesses in low-income areas, making this city one of the national leaders in the industry.

Some people are open books. As a former army infantryman, Ph.D. in biochemistry, real-estate developer and patron of the arts, Bob Gerding is an encyclopedia. Gerding/Edlen Development Company owned the Armory and, though other profitable opportunities existed, made the critical decision to create a new theater out of this historic structure. No doubt Bob appreciates the symmetry of creating an arts center from an armory, and his passion for creating a meaningful asset for the community that has given him so much over the years is a powerful statement from a deeply thoughtful and courageous man.

I think you'll be amused to read Chris Coleman's first impression of former Mayor Vera Katz. Her central role in this project is undeniable. It was Vera who made the critical political stand to preserve the Armory, as she had many other historic buildings in the city. As a long-time champion of the arts, she supported moving Portland Center Stage to the building. "Make it happen," she told me four years ago. And if you've ever met Vera, you know that when she tells you to do something, you figure out a way to get it done.

The heart of this group is Julie Vigeland. She was chair of Portland Center Stage when the project began, and now chairs the Armory Theater Fund capital campaign. From beginning to end, Julie's vigorous spirit and relentless search for solutions has inspired us all to help the stars align.

A note about the narrative structure:

In honor of the primary use of the Gerding Theater at the Armory, this book is structured like a play. The main character is Chris Coleman, artistic director of Portland Center Stage. His story is a personal one about the trials and tribulations of the project from one of his first visits to Portland until just a few months ago. I think you'll agree that he's quite a storyteller and offers the singular perspective of an artistic director trying to move mountains (politicians, investors, city planners, developers and me, to name a few) for his company. It is a tale about regional theater; artistic, financial and political risk; civic and architectural foresight; money; sustainability; and Portland. It is a tale, most of all, about this community.

The technical expertise needed to create a new building within a century-old structure with a LEED Platinum sustainability achievement has been extraordinary. Rather than ask Chris to recite the minutiae of excavation, natural ventilation and tax-credit finance (though at this point, he probably could), we've arranged for a chorus of "voices" to assist him. This catalogue of 50 voices from the front lines of this epic project — and a few from the outside — forms a fascinating historical record of the experience and expertise, drama and energy needed to make something truly wonderful happen.

The score for our play comes in the form of images by local photographers who documented the entire construction process. These act as a sort of visual timeline throughout the book to accompany the text.

We hope you will enjoy *Voices of the Armory* and visit Portland's newest — and oldest and greenest — theater again and again. Enjoy!

A CENTURY IN PORTLAND:
Through the Lens of the Armory

BART KING

16,000 BCE

Massive floods from melting inland glaciers pour through the Willamette Valley, and the future site of the Armory is submerged 400 feet underwater. After this sluicing, primeval forest again takes root.

1500-1600S CE

Douglas fir saplings in the Willamette Valley begin growing into the trees that will eventually be cut down to form the Armory's trusses.

1803

The United States purchases the Louisiana Territory from France, and Oregon is included in the deal. In a short while Lewis and Clark will pass through the area.

1830s

Travelers on the Willamette use the future site of Portland as a rest stop. As historian Terence O'Donnell later observed, *"there are certain things that you cannot do from a canoe."*

1843

With new immigrants now arriving via the Oregon Trail, business partners William Overton and Asa Lovejoy claim 640 acres on the west bank of the Willamette River. Two years and one coin toss later, it's named "Portland."

1846

The Portland plat establishes a downtown design of 16 city blocks. Portland's population is about 800. The city streets are all dirt (or mud), filled with stumps, and planks are used for sidewalks, hence the city's moniker, "Stumptown."

1848

Congress passes the Oregon "Organic Act," creating the Oregon Territory (and presaging future organic co-ops in the city).

1856

A young German immigrant named Henry Weinhard moves to Portland and (with partner George Bottler) establishes Portland's second brewery.

1859

Oregon achieves statehood. (As Oregonians had previously voted three times against becoming a state, there is little rejoicing.)

1864

Henry Weinhard opens a brewery building just southwest of the Armory's future location. (*Now* there's rejoicing.)

1870

Chinatown is established south of Burnside. Portland's population is about 8,000.

1873

A fire at the corner of First Avenue and Salmon Street, destroys 20 downtown blocks. Armory architect Richard Martin arrives in Portland from Penzance, England the following year.

1882

Dublin-born architect William F. McCaw, who will later join Martin in designing the Armory annex, moves to Portland from Toronto.

1887

After considerable violence against the local Chinese population, Oregon authorizes the building of armories to allow for the drilling and practice of the National Guard. A quote from Judge George H. Williams in his speech at the construction site illustrates the need for such a building: *"Communists, socialists, and nihilists — the enemies of God and man — are swarming...to this free land, and with diabolical zeal are working up an organized hostility to the reign of law and the rights of property...citizens should organize themselves...to uphold...the cause of law and order."*

1888

The first Portland Armory is completed to architect Richard Martin's designs and is almost immediately found to be too small. Colonel Charles F. Beebe, great-grandfather of Spencer (of Ecotrust renown), is its first officer. Also this year, the Skidmore Fountain is dedicated, and Portland is first named the "City of Roses."

1890

The Portland Hotel opens at the present site of Pioneer Courthouse Square. The city's first electric streetcars begin operation. Portland's population is about 46,000 (5,200 are Chinese).

1891

Architects McCaw and Martin's "annex" to the Armory is completed. (This is the building we think of as the Armory today.) A crowd of 5,000 attends the dedication ceremony.

1896

Union Station opens.

1898

Soldiers are mustered in the Armory for the Spanish-American War.

1900

City population: 90,426. The Armory is filled to capacity to honor war dead lying in flag-draped coffins as the Portland Symphony Orchestra performs.

1903

Lillian Nordica performs a concert at the Armory with the Duss Orchestra. *The Oregonian* reports that "three thousand people...listened to and applauded Madame Nordica...[who] looked like the grand opera Queen that she is."

1905

The Lewis and Clark Exposition welcomes 2.5 million visitors to Portland, spurring the city's development.

1907

Queen Flora presides over Portland's first Rose Festival. She is joined the following year by a king with a fake beard — "Rex Oregonus." The Society Circus performs at the Armory, and a local paper reports, "peanut shells fell like snow drops and lemonade flowed like water." Later this year, John Philip Sousa performs at the Armory. *The Oregonian* calls it "one of, if not in fact the very finest, evenings Portland has ever spent with a band of music."

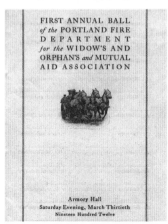

FIRST ANNUAL BALL
of the PORTLAND FIRE
DEPARTMENT
for the WIDOW'S AND
ORPHAN'S *and* MUTUAL
AID ASSOCIATION

Armory Hall
Saturday Evening, March Thirtieth
Nineteen Hundred Twelve

MEETING in honor of the President of the United States, at the Armory, Portland, Oregon, Saturday, October 2, 1909, at 8 o'clock

Admit Mr._____
TO PRESS SEAT

Entrance East or Tenth Street door.
This ticket must be shown at rope and door entrances.

SOUVENIR

1908

Weinhard's Brewery gets a new Tuscan-style building. Prohibition-era attitudes will soon bring trouble for Weinhard's, with local politician Oswald West stating, *"There isn't a brick in the brewery down here that doesn't represent a broken heart."*

1910

City population: 207,214, more than double that of the previous decade. A Women's Christian Temperance Union event causes the smashing of many bottles of liquor, and Walter Damrosch and the New York Symphony play two shows at the Armory later in the year.

1911

Former president Theodore Roosevelt, acting president William Howard Taft and future president Woodrow Wilson all give speeches at the Armory on separate occasions. Roosevelt later lays the cornerstone of the Multnomah Athletic Club. Additional Armory events include the Russian Symphony Orchestra of New York, and a concert by opera diva Mary Garden.

1912

The first Benson Bubblers are installed downtown. A city commission finds that more than 80% of the city's 547 hotels and boarding houses are houses of ill repute.

1916

Oregon officially becomes a "dry" state three years before Prohibition kicks in nationally. Soldiers are soon to be mustered in the Armory for World War I.

1919

The first US Amateur Men's boxing matches are held at the Armory; the main event pits Joe Gorman (a.k.a. the "Spanish Tamale") against Hector St. John. (The Tamale wins.) Boxing matches continue being held at the Armory until 1937.

1920

General John "Black Jack" Pershing, leader of the Allied Expeditionary Force in the First World War, addressed a crowd of more than 3,000 ex-service men and women at the Armory, proclaiming that Oregon soldiers were "second to none."

1921

A rowdy crowd of 1,500 veterans gather at the Armory for an American Legion meeting. They pass a resolution calling on the state legislature to allow veterans the choice of $25 for each month of military service or a $3,000 home or farm loan.

1924

Dozens of teens are arrested for disturbing Armory boxing crowds and vandalizing the building.

1926

The Oregon National Guard holds public demonstrations in the Armory of bayonet exercises, machine gun drills and a howitzer platoon in action. A dance follows.

1928

The Portland Kennel Club holds their dog show at the Armory. Later that year, Olympic wrestling trials are held here. Portland fire marshal Fred W. Roberts states that *"the Armory is a fire hazard and always has been."*

1930

American Legion Circus Maximus is held at the Armory. *The Oregonian* described the acts as coming "from the aristocracy of circus talent... Leo, the Metro-Goldwyn-Mayer lion, who growls an introduction to all his producer's photoplays, is to start New Year's by making Portland a visit as a guest star." "Hoovervilles" (homes made of corrugated tin and tar paper) begin appearing in Sullivan's Gulch, where Highway 84 now runs. City population is about 300,000.

1933

In an apparent act of defiance to Portland fire marshal Fred W. Roberts' 1928 statement, more than 2,000 Camp Fire Girls meet at the Armory to hold their grand council fire.

1938

The Armory is used as a site to handle unemployment claims.

1946

Portland State University founded. Along with the University of Portland, the schools' basketball teams will sometimes compete in the Armory.

1948

The Armory takes in refugees from the huge Vanport flood. (Vanport was located where East and West Delta Parks are today.) Audiences at the Armory watch the Portland Indians defeat the Seattle Athletics to take the Pacific Coast Professional Basketball League Championship.

1950

City population is about 370,000. Portland's last streetcar goes out of service.

1953

Big Time Wrestling premieres on KPTV and remains a hit for nearly two decades. Bronco Nagurski, one of the greatest football players in collegiate grid history, took the spotlight in the top attraction of the Portland Wrestling Club's mat show at the Armory, appearing in a seven-man battle royal.

1952

The Portland Hotel is demolished to make way for a parking lot.

1954

Matt Groening, creator of *The Simpsons*, is born in Portland.

1956

Pinball machines are outlawed in Portland for the next two decades.

1960

Lloyd Center opens. It is the nation's largest, urban shopping center at this time.

1962

The Armory hosts exhibition matches between some of the world's great tennis pros, Jack Kramer and Bobby Riggs among them. The Columbus Day Storm lashes the city with nature's fury.

1965

The Godfather of Soul, James Brown, headlines at the Portland Armory with his big 18-piece band plus The Famous Flames, Bobby Byrd, James Crawford, Baby Lloyd, Al "Briscoe" Clark and "TV Mama" Elsie Mae.

1968-69

The Blitz-Weinhard Brewing Company purchases the Armory as a warehouse and bottling plant for $302,600. A conveyor belt is installed over 11th Avenue. The historic archway over the door on the 11th Avenue entrance is torn off and a 14' x 14' garage door is installed to allow the passage of beer trucks. The original 1887 Armory is demolished for a parking lot. The architectural firm Rudat, Boutwell & Associates opens; the partnership name will eventually morph into GBD Architects in 1991.

1970

City population about 380,000. This decade sees the whitewashing of the Armory's exterior.

1971

Powell's Books opens one block south of the Armory on the derelict corner of a former car dealership.

1974

Demolition begins on Harbor Drive so that Waterfront Park can be constructed.

1977

The Portland Trail Blazers win the National Basketball Association championship.

1979

The Blitz-Weinhard Brewery is sold to the Miller Brewing Company. (The Armory continues in its former capacity under new management.)

1980

Mount St. Helens erupts. Portland's population is about 370,000.

1984

Pioneer Courthouse Square opens. Personalized bricks in the square include Bertha D. Blues, God, Frodo Baggins and Mr. Spock.

1986

MAX light rail begins operations.

1987

The term "Pearl District" is coined to describe the Northwest neighborhood's plethora of crusty warehouses filled with art.

1988

The Oregonian writer Ken Wheeler describes the Armory as *"two places deep on the downside of prime."*

1990

City population: 438,802. (This significant gain comes one year after the premiere of *The Simpsons*. Coincidence?)

1993

Portland Center Stage becomes an independent theater company.

1999

The Armory is purchased by the Gerding/Edlen Development Company as part of the Brewery Blocks package.

2000

The Armory is placed on the National Register of Historic Places.

2001

Portland's "Office of Sustainable Development" is formed.

2001

In his last legislative act in office, President William J. Clinton signs the New Markets Tax Credits program into law to stimulate private business investment in qualifying census tracts. The Armory will become one of the first major projects in the country to make use of the tax credits program.

2002

Bob Gerding first suggests the Armory as a possible home for Portland Center Stage. Portland Family of Funds is formed with Norris Lozano as CEO and president, and Ed Jensen, Ralph Shaw and Carl Talton among the board of directors.

2003

The Portland Development Commission approves a loan for the purchase and redevelopment of the Armory.

2004

The Armory transaction closes and construction begins. The Henry, a 15-story condominium tower, opens adjacent to the Armory.

2005

$8.1 million is raised to ensure that the Armory will achieve the highest standards in green construction. The money is also used to fully fund the design and building of adjacent Sliver Park (recently renamed Vera Katz Park), as well as a community-oriented lobby, with multimedia displays by Portland's Second Story Interactive Studios.

2006

West Side Story opens at the newly titled Gerding Theater at the Armory. It is the first building on the National Register of Historic Places — and the first theater — to achieve a "Platinum" Leadership in Energy and Environmental Design (LEED) rating from the US Green Building Council.

Meanwhile, Douglas fir saplings continue growing in the Willamette Valley.

IT'S A VAST SPACE, EMPTY AND SILENT. I'D GUES
THE DIMENSIONS TO BE 100' X 200' – MAYBE BIGGE
THE FLOOR IS CONCRETE BUT COVERED IN DII
WITH BIG PUDDLES OF WATER IN SUNKEN AREA
ABOVE OUR HEADS, HUGE, SOARING BEAM
STRETCH ACROSS A ROOF THE WIDTH OF
FOOTBALL FIELD. NOT A SOUL IN SIGHT — WEL
ACTUALLY, TWO HAPPY PIGEONS HAVE NESTE
AMONG THE TRUSSES. AND NOT A SINGLE COLUM
OBSTRUCTS THE BUILDING'S CENTRAL EXPANS
IT IS STUNNING.

WE STAND FOR SEVERAL MOMENTS IN SILENC
LISTENING TO THE TRAFFIC MOVE PAST. THEN
TURN TO CREON AND SAY: "HEY: THIS LOOK
LIKE A THEATER."

CH:1

CHRIS
COLEMAN

SETTING THE STAGE:
An Abandoned Warehouse Waits

IN THIS CHAPTER

An Atlanta theater director and the old abandoned Portland Armory meet. A complicated courtship begins, and the soon-to-be Portland Center Stage artistic director starts a four-year journey into Portland's cultural and urban development.

FIRST SIGHTING I'm riding in a green Ford Ranger with Creon Thorne, production manager at Portland Center Stage, on my third trip to Portland. It is drizzling, the streets are slick, and we are rambling through an area of downtown that reminds me of SoHo in the 1970s (before there was a Prada store). It's October of 1999, and most of the buildings are pretty beat up: old warehouses have boarded up windows, the Weinhard Brewery sits empty and Whole Foods is only an idea waiting to find life on Northwest Couch Street. But Powell's Books is around the corner, and a few new buildings are under construction down the street. I'm in town for my final interview for the job of artistic director at Center Stage, the idea of finding a new home has surfaced, and Creon has a space he wants to show me.

We park beside an old building on NW 11th Avenue and Davis Street. Its brick walls have been painted white, there are funny turrets on the exterior corners, and you can see slots that were clearly designed to let a rifle poke through (protecting someone from something, I guess). The structure inhabits half a city block, and while it was likely imposing in its day, it is probably no more than 35 or 40 feet high. Climbing out of the truck, we survey the building. There are no signs that say "Keep Out," and neither of us is particularly shy, so we poke our heads inside.

It's a vast space, empty and silent. I'd guess the dimensions to be 100' x 200' – maybe bigger.

First Sighting *continued*

The floor is concrete but covered in dirt with big puddles of water in sunken areas. Above our heads, huge, soaring beams stretch across a roof the width of a football field. Not a soul is in sight — well, actually, two happy pigeons have nested among the trusses. And not a single column obstructs the building's central expanse. It is stunning.

We stand for several moments in silence, listening to the traffic move past. Then I turn to Creon and say: "Hey: this looks like a theater."

The Armory is fascinating for having survived repeated attempts over 110 years to either abandon it or to tear it down. On the one hand, the structure was adapted to suit a variety of needs, and as a result, it established itself as a fixture in the neighborhood. On the other, it seems that no matter how many times the Armory faced the wrecking ball, no one could actually demolish it. The building hung on just long enough to get a new lease on life, and to my mind, it's a good thing that it did.

Bob Kingston. Historian

THE GERM

The idea of converting the 100-year-old Portland Armory into a new home for Portland Center Stage actually began with a question: "How can a major regional theater reinvent its relationship to its community in the 21st century?" It wasn't a question that the characters in this story came to in a theoretical way. In fact, I think each of us arrived at the question from very different histories and experiences. What we shared was a love of theater and a desire to see the art form influence our community in a more meaningful way.

Theater is about sharing stories. It is, as a friend of mine once said, "about gathering a community around a campfire" and sharing tales of our loves, conquests, betrayals, pratfalls, victories, failures and fears. And since the moment in 437 B.C., when the first Greek actor stepped out of a chorus and began "embodying the story," each generation of theater-makers has reinvented both the way their stories were told (the dramatic form of the play) and the architecture within which the stories were shared. My strong sense at the time was that in the 20th century, American playwrights had made great strides in catching up with the spirit of our time. But theaters themselves, the physical spaces in which we engage our community, were stuck. I believed that the key to discovering a more dynamic relationship with our audience lay in thinking more creatively, more irreverently, more bluntly about how people experience the building in which we share stories. And I was looking for a chance to try something different.

> Nearly upon completion, the First Regiment outgrew its original building and plans for an annex began. The new hall featured a wood-truss roof system that provided a 100-foot north-south clear-span that not only allowed military drills but also concerts and even baseball games. Around the perimeter was a mezzanine gallery with space for audiences of 5,000. The National Guard used the Armory for the next 80 years.
>
> *John Tess,* Principal, Heritage Consulting

MY MOST VIVID MEMORY IS OF...WRESTLING. DON AND ELTON OWEN WRESTLING. TOM PETERSON KNOCKING ON YOUR TV SCREEN WRESTLING. BARNEY KEEP WISECRACKING IN THE "CROW'S NEST" WRESTLING. THE PURISTS PRONOUNCED IT "RASSLIN'." MY FATHER NEVER FAILED TO REFER TO IT AS "GRUNT AND GROAN."

John Terry. Columnist, *The Oregonian*

The Germ *continued*

For me, the search really began out of boredom. Slight backtrack. Prior to my move to Portland in May of 2000, I had been running a small theater in Atlanta. It was a company I founded in the basement of an old church in 1988 with Harold Leaver, a buddy from high school. We pretended we had $5,000 and went around talking to people for three months trying to figure out what it would take to get a season off the ground. "How much would it cost to rent the chairs? How about the lighting instruments? If we filled half the house how much could we earn? A quarter of the house? Who do you send a press release to?" We ended up in the church basement because, though the most difficult location to market, it was cheap as dirt ($200 per production), already had seats and a few lights and we could paint sets in the parking lot. Those were heady days.

We had a great run of it at Actor's Express and after twelve years had produced everything from Shakespeare to Tony Kushner, building our budget to almost $800,000. We won a slew of awards for

The Germ *continued*

acting and directing: "Best Theatre" by *Creative Loafing* (the weekly alternative newspaper) from 1995-1997, and "Outstanding Arts Organization" by the Chamber of Commerce in 1998. Artistic directors from larger theaters around the country had flown to town to see the work, and our success had brought invitations for me to direct in Dallas, Pittsburgh, Baltimore, Seattle, New York and Ashland.

Thoughts of running a bigger theater had been bubbling in my head for a while. The attraction was the notion of having more resources: access to a higher caliber of actor and designer on a more consistent basis, and the opportunity to have a larger "congregation" to speak to. But taking over just any regional theater didn't sound so interesting; it had to be the right opportunity. Because for me, many of the big, regional theaters had become so mired in their success at creating an institution that the work onstage, and the way audiences got to experience that work, bored the pants off me.

What do I mean? If you could travel back to 1945 and look at the professional theater in America, you would see 12 blocks of real estate on Broadway...if you wanted to see a professional play you had to travel to New York. To most people working in the theater, that didn't seem right.

Chris Coleman

What do I mean? If you could travel back to 1945 and look at the professional theater in America, you would see 12 blocks of real estate on Broadway. That was it. The success of the television and film industries had decimated the thriving stock and touring companies that had been so prevalent in the United States in the early part of the twentieth century. So, if you wanted to see a professional play you had to travel to New York. To most people working in the theater, that didn't seem right.

The Germ *continued*

Then just after World War II several key players began to imagine a different scenario. One of those individuals was the famous stage director of the 1920s and 30s, Arthur Hopkins (probably best known as the director of John Barrymore's *Hamlet*). In 1948 he gave a series of lectures at Fordham University that described his vision of a succession of fully professionalized repertory companies located in every city in America. He imagined a company of professional actors, producers and craftspeople who would live in the same city as their audience members. He imagined an audience that would commit to a theater over many years, reveling in the opportunity to consider a whole body of work. And he imagined theaters that would bring the great works of dramatic literature as well as the voices of new playwrights to Americans in San Francisco, Kansas City, Seattle, etc. The lectures were captured in a book entitled *Reference Point* (Samuel French, 1949), and as I left for college in 1979, my mother (an actress) slipped a copy into my suitcase.

When Hopkins delivered his lectures at Fordham, only a handful of regional theaters existed outside of New York City, each striving toward fully professional status. Today there are more than 1,600 nonprofit theaters of every shape, size and description in virtually every city across our land — maybe 60 of which you could describe as "flagship theaters." And as the first wave of "regional" theaters began to establish themselves in Washington, D.C., Houston and Minneapolis during the mid-1950s, they fought hard and assiduously to procure a significant level of support and respect in their communities. As Zelda Fichandler, the legendary founder of Arena Stage in D.C. said, "We wanted a place at the table like the hospital and the university, and the library. We wanted to be viewed as institutions that were worth investing in over time" (*Preserving the Legacy*, Vol. I, DVD, TCG Publications, 2003).

The movement succeeded radically. The "flagship" regional theaters found audiences, built repertoires, constructed buildings, took plays to Broadway, trained new artists, created boards of directors, launched new play festivals, and established endowments. These big regional theaters indeed succeeded in becoming institutions, enabling them to survive the succession of their founders and to contribute to a community over the long haul. And with that success came all the downsides of institutionalization. The organizations became big, unwieldy, conservative, and slow to respond to the rapidly shifting cultural trends reshaping how we process information and experience our lives in the 21st century.

> Think about it. We dress up like we're going to church, we walk into the lobby, have a drink, wait till they flash the lights, file into a room together, wait till the lights go out, sit quietly — laugh on occasion (if we're lucky) — and applaud at the end. Nothing wrong with that. But this is basically the same way we were experiencing theater 100 years ago...Where was the sense of adventure? Of event? Of participation?
>
> *Chris Coleman*

The Germ *continued*

Think about it. You can still go to the big theaters and find great work onstage — but how do we get to experience that work? We dress up like we're going to church, we walk into the lobby, have a drink, wait till they flash the lights, file into a room together, wait till the lights go out, sit quietly — laugh on occasion (if we're lucky) and applaud at the end. Nothing wrong with that. But this is basically the same way we were experiencing theater 100 years ago. Perhaps it's the best way. But it feels awfully static, grown-up, and predictable to me. Where was the sense of adventure? Of event? Of participation? Where was the vitality I saw at the Farmer's Market, at the Blues Festival, or at Jameson Square, or on "myspace.com"— or heck, even at Starbucks?

So yes, I wanted to run a bigger theater, but I really longed for the opportunity to work with a group of people who were willing to throw the balls up in the air and see if there wasn't a more fun way of doing things. What did "fun" look like? I wasn't sure yet, but I knew that it had

The Germ *continued*

something to do with the "experience" of theater exploding outside the traditional walls of the theaters themselves.

Enter Portland Center Stage.

When we met, PCS was already a flagship regional theater, but the unique story of its birth had made the company's need to reexamine its operating model more than a theoretical curiosity. Center Stage came about because a handful of theater lovers sat down over drinks at a pub in Ashland (home of the renowned Oregon Shakespeare Festival) and asked, "What would it take to have theater of this quality in Portland?" About the same time, Portland Center for the Performing Arts was in search of an anchor tenant for its new theater building. After many months of study, fundraising and political maneuvering, in 1987, the Oregon Shakespeare Festival decided to launch an adjunct operation: OSF Portland. It is important to note that the OSF Board decision passed by one vote, and the artistic director at the time, Jerry Turner,

was against any dilution of the company's operation. Neither was a promising sign.

Despite the initial reluctance, the first few years (1988-1994) saw artistic successes and enormous excitement for the new theater company, operating as a satellite of the mother ship. But OSF was losing about $350,000 a year on the Portland experiment, and after five years, it gracefully decided to hand the operation over to what until then had been a group of community advisors, making them the board of directors in the process, and forming an independent company: Portland Center Stage.

Which must have been thrilling. And terrifying. After five years, they were the big game in town, had a big, beautiful theater (almost 900 seats) and a subscription base that far outnumbered the next-largest theater. But the company also had a budget of $2.2 million a year.

Now — anyone who is a student of the regional theater operating model could tell you pretty quickly that if you are successfully operating a 900-seat theater, you are likely in a city with a population base of four million or more, and you have an annual operating budget somewhere between $12 and $20 million. You are most likely a company that has been in business for many years. Your audience has grown gradually along with you, so that together you are ready to fill those seats. So trying to make this very exciting "flagship theater" sail in a city of 1.5 million people, with a tiny budget, and a very young audience base was a challenge indeed.

My predecessor, Elizabeth Huddle, had had a brilliant career as an actress in San Francisco, and then led Intiman Theatre in Seattle, prior to taking the reins at PCS. Liz decided, after seven valiant years, that she had fought the battle long enough and would retire.

The Board of Directors at PCS were looking for both new leadership and a way to make the company artistically and economically viable. This is when we met: the board and I, both of us searching.

And I'll admit that the courtship took a moment. I loved Portland from the first time I drove through town, but anybody in his right mind would have looked at the challenges the theater faced and thought twice, or three times, before saying yes to the job. But there were some unique and very persuasive people on the search committee, including most critically Julie Vigeland (board chair at the time); and Bob Gerding (the board's vice chair for development).

During the search process, the headhunter asked me to write down the shows I might produce during the first three seasons. I thought that was a bunch of hooey, so I just decided to write down the craziest ideas that popped into my head. I think I said we should do *Betty's Summer Vacation* (Christopher Durang's wildly funny, and wildly perverse satire about American media); a production of *La Boheme* (ax the chorus; use rehearsal clothes, the eight principals and one piano; no set — hey this actually still sounds pretty cool); *Once in a Lifetime* (Kaufman and Hart's screwball comedy requiring a cast of, like 50); Nancy Keystone's original multimedia version of *Antigone*; and *The Devils* (Elizabeth Egloff's dark, delicious, epic treatment of Dostoyevsky's novel). Honestly I thought I would scare

> During the search process, the headhunter asked me to write down the shows I might produce during the first three seasons...I decided to write down the craziest ideas that popped into my head. I think I said we should do *Betty's Summer Vacation*, *La Boheme*; *Once in a Lifetime*; Nancy Keystone's original multi-media version of *Antigone*; and Elizabeth Egloff's *The Devils*. Honestly, I thought I would scare them off.
>
> *Chris Coleman*

them off. And if I didn't — well, then, maybe this Portland gig was worth a real conversation. The head-hunter called me back and said the committee was totally jazzed by the list. Doy. In fact, every time I called attention to an obstacle we would face (including building a new home for the company) the committee seemed to get more excited. It became very clear that they were hungry to make something significant happen with this theater company and that they were willing to take bold action to bring that about. I believe Bob Gerding's statement was, "We're either going to make this theater successful, or we're going to burn it down." That kind of hunger was just what I was looking for.

It was during my second interview that I had a chance to sit privately with Mr. Gerding and learn about why he was so committed to the future of Portland. Bob is the founding principal in Gerding/Edlen Development, among the most successful real-estate development companies in Oregon. He looks like the former football player (at Portland's Lincoln High) that he is, and his presence is hard to miss in a room.

You definitely want Bob on your side in a disagreement, but when he gets excited he turns into a big seven year old. He has one of the most deeply complex intellects I have encountered and can hold forth at length about anything from the brain's chemical reaction to proteins to proper technique for fly fishing to the inner meaning of Rumi's poems. He is also genuinely moved by the art form of theater.

Bob talked about his career as a biochemist and his decision at age 50 to move into real-estate development because he wanted to make a difference in the life of the city that meant so much to him. He talked about how theater had influenced him since his teacher Ruth Arbuckle made him play one of the witches in *Macbeth* his senior year at Lincoln. He talked about how he believed theater was the "campfire" around which a community gathered to share its stories, and how his experiences with plays over the years had fed him spiritually.

...the building is already brilliantly theatrical and innately compelling. In its pre-renovation form it was: dirt floor; cavernous; sweeping overhead trusses; old brick; stone and mortar; outside turrets and towers; arched entrances; mysterious apertures — gun ports; windows; and who knows what — a combination of solid mass and air.

Nancy Keystone. Theater Director, Writer, Visual Artist

And at the end of our meeting he said, "I don't know if you are going to take this job or not. But I like listening to you talk, and wherever you go, I'd like to follow your career. But if you do take the job, I will help you find the resources to make it successful." That was the critical statement in compelling me to leave my family, my friends, my partner and the company I had founded to move across the country. And that statement will prove to be the keystone in the story you are reading about the Portland Armory.

GROUNDWORK

During my first two years at PCS, forward motion on "The Armory Project," as we called it, was on the backburner. From time to time, Creon and I would cruise by and see if anybody had laid claim to it. Or Bob might casually mention how cool it would be as a theater. But it wasn't a serious focus of our energy. We had plenty of other things to worry about.

Those first two seasons were about laying groundwork to strengthen the theater's operations and financial base. We needed more resources if we were going to deliver the goods a "flagship theater" ought to be offering its community. But we couldn't expect more resources until we had a clear plan in place and were able to articulate what a higher level of investment might yield. I knew that delivering a first-rate product and building our audience were both going to require more funding than we could currently attract.

One example: actor salaries. Coming from tiny Actor's Express, I expected that if you went to New York to audition actors and were able to offer $625

Groundwork *continued*

a week you could get whomever you wanted. What I quickly learned was that a New Yorker can't pay his rent on that salary, so we were sometimes getting our 2nd, 3rd or 4th choices in a casting session. I was also interested in making it easier for talented local actors to stay in Portland. To make sure the work onstage excelled, we had to pay more.

During that first season a small group of board and staff members worked with arts consultant George Thorne to draft the theater's first strategic plan. It was comprehensive and ambitious. We spoke of wanting to become a home for new work, a theater that developed deep relationships with artists over time, and a center for dialogue in the community. We wanted to attract a younger, more diverse audience, to develop educational programs, to forge international relationships and to become a theater that was consistently able to produce work of the highest caliber. We also expressed a strong desire to create a home for this work, a home that would invite the community in during many hours of the day. We wanted to build a place where you might

hang out and have a cup of coffee, bring your kid to an acting class, or stay late for a jazz concert; a building with fantastic perform-ance spaces, yes, but would also be a fun place to socialize. The strategic plan envisioned construction of this new home as the final chapter of Phase I of our work, and at the time it seemed a distant dream.

In terms of how to calibrate our change of direction onstage, those early days were about "taking the temperature" of the audience. My sense from the search committee and core staff was that to resonate with Portland, PCS had to be producing work that spoke to our time. Why not just do the kind of work that Ashland had been doing? (Because they were already doing a pretty good job of that!) We had to figure out how to be a theater for Portland. The city had become one of the most forward-thinking com-munities in the country, and that had meant a willingness to take a controversial stand or two. So if we were to create a theater that really excited this particular community, we had to be willing to shake things up from time to time.

Of course we could produce classics, but we needed to do so with a particularly strong point-of-view. But we should also be doing the best new material coming out of London and New York (PCS had passed on *Wit*, *Gross Indecency*, *Arcadia* and *Love! Valour! Compassion!* allowing other Portland theaters to pick up these excellent plays). We should be developing wholly original work and producing it on our stage. And we should be mounting musicals — both old-fashioned chestnuts that blaze in a good production, and the smart, sophisticated groundbreakers coming from the likes of William Finn and Jeanine Tesori. So in we jumped.

I had weighed many ideas for our inaugural production and landed on Elizabeth Egloff's adaptation of Dostoyevsky's novel *The Devils*. It's a sprawling, three-act piece that centers on a slapdash band of would-be revolutionaries who are manipulated into disastrous action

WE OPENED TO AN AMAZING REVIEW... IN *THE OREGONIAN*...BUT THE RESPONSES WERE NOT ALL SO WARM. I VIVIDLY REMEMBER A PHONE CALL OUR RECEPTIONIST TOOK DURING THE SHOW FROM A WOMAN WHO SAID, "WELL IF THIS IS THE KIND OF STUFF HE'S GOING TO DO, TELL HIM TO GO BACK TO ATLANTA.

Chris Coleman   p40

Groundwork *continued*

by a cunning young anarchist. I loved the play's sweep, humor, scenic complexity, and rich humanity. The text does employ adult language, and climaxes with the revelation that the dissolute former leader of the band raped a young girl while in Berlin. This key chapter in Dostoyevsky's original was not allowed in print until the 1950s — and the scene that Egloff devised for the revelation was heart-stopping and chilling. At a running time of three hours and fifteen minutes it is a banquet and a half — but I felt the production would also signal a willingness to make bold theatrical choices and that the company was marching in a vivid new direction.

We opened to an amazing review by Bob Hicks in *The Oregonian* who seemed to clearly understand what we were about. But the responses were not all so warm. I vividly remember a phone call our receptionist took during the show from a woman who said, "Well if this is the kind of stuff he's going to do, tell him to go back to Atlanta." None of us had quite realized how quickly we were moving in relation to where the rest of the audience was sitting.

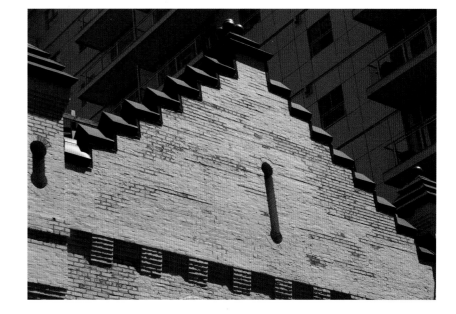

Groundwork *continued*

Suffice it to say, we lost subscribers, we lost some donors, we got letters. Who knew that so many people cared about the theater? At the same time, we were starting to find new subscribers, to see a trickle of younger ticket buyers walk in the door, and we were also gaining attention from friends around the city who had never looked our way.

Two critical events occurred during that early period. In January of 2001 we appealed to the city for operating support to help make the transition with our audience, and the following fall we procured a major grant from the Meyer Memorial Trust, a leading Portland private foundation.

Prior to my arrival, the Art Museum, Ballet, Opera and Symphony had all received grants of $200,000 a year for five years from the mayor's office, but because PCS had never quite made it into the category of the "majors," we hadn't yet benefited.

After working hard to prove our commitment and value to the arts community with the City Council and Mayor Vera Katz, we received appropriations during my first two seasons (before the economy headed south). To some observers in Portland, these gifts were controversial. Coming from Atlanta, where all the major arts organizations receive $150,000 per year (or more depending on the size of their budget) from *each* of the city, county and state governments — I was a bit taken aback that you had to lobby so hard to get a single gift.

The critical event here was meeting Mayor Katz. And what a meeting. Having spent so many years in the South, I was accustomed to mayors who resembled Baptist preachers: big on noise and small on action. In my first meeting with Vera, she strode in with her sparkly eyes and said, "OK you have half an hour. What are you going to do for Portland?" I was knocked out by how real and cool and cute she was (and yes, at 68 she was still cute). I mean, if you had to have a mayor, why shouldn't she be funny and focused and smart? This initial introduction would prove pivotal to the project's success.

On the heels of our strategic plan, we drafted a proposal to the Meyer Memorial Trust, requesting a grant of $1.35 million over three years to help us put stronger work onstage. Our argument was that if we could convince the community to make a larger investment in the company, we had a chance of creating a platform from which to set the company's long-term financial equation aright.

In November of 2001, we produced the world premiere of *Flesh and Blood*, an adaptation of Michael Cunningham's epic novel about an American family. Cunningham had just won the Pulitzer for *The Hours*, and it was a thrill to work on his story of a Greek immigrant who comes to America in 1935 to build his fortune and his family. *Flesh and Blood* tracks America's path through the sexual revolution of the 1960s, the AIDS crisis of the 1980s, and finally lands in 2035. A lush, sexy, and wrenching landscape emerges — and it lands on the audience with great power. I was very proud that we had helped the adaptor (Peter Gaitens) hone the piece in our new play festival, Just Add Water/West, the prior summer. Despite the racy nature of the play's content, it handily exceeded its box-office goal and was subsequently produced at New York Theater Workshop. It seemed we were beginning to find the theater's "new" audience.

> Having spent so many years in the South, I was accustomed to mayors who resembled Baptist preachers: big on noise and small on action. In my first meeting with Vera, she strode in with piercing eyes and said, "OK you have half an hour. What are you going to do for Portland?
>
> *Chris Coleman*

Groundwork *continued*

That same month, the Meyer Trust, said "yes" — issuing a challenge grant for the full amount requested. It was the largest grant PCS had ever received, and the largest the Trust would award to an arts organization for another four years. This grant and the campaign we built around it, were huge milestones, helping us take our case to the community in a much more visible way.

When I was a lad of 12 or so, the Armory used to be the home of Portland Wrestling, broadcasting live every Saturday night on Channel 12. My friends and I were huge fans of this most theatrical of athletic events. We would dress up as our heroes — Lonnie "Moondog" Mayne, Beauregard, Dutch Savage, Shag Thomas — and parade around our houses during the show.

Somehow we talked our way into the arena, and during a break in the action, we jumped in the ring. Two of us mimicked our idols, while two of us held a large banner declaring "LONNIE MAYNE AND BEAUREGARD ARE WORLD CHAMPS!" The authorities quickly rounded us up and escorted us out of the building, but not before we were on TV, live, for the benefit of our dear mothers back home.

Jamey Hampton. Artistic Director, BodyVox

THE SECOND STORY ABOUT THE ARMORY

Design Firm Provides Context

ARMORY VOICES:
Design

BRAD
JOHNSON

Several years ago our studio created a popular website for Egyptologist Kent Weeks, who spent his life documenting the Valley of the Kings and the entire Theban Necropolis. His motto was: "Preservation begins with documentation." The thinking is that the more people know about something, the more motivated they will be to protect and preserve it. Since then, the interactive media we create has helped document, interpret and "protect" a rural eighteenth-century Chinese home, a whaling ship, Thomas Jefferson's Monticello, our native forests and thousands of artifacts and objects in museum collections around the world. • Helping audiences better connect with things of cultural, environmental and historical significance has been the most rewarding work we do — and until the Portland Armory we have never had an opportunity to apply our craft to a single project in which all three of these elements came together in one package. The building has a rich and diverse history; its current transformation is considerate of the environment; and its theatrical incarnation will contribute to the culture of our community indefinitely. • In a kind of media midwifery, we helped the Armory let its stories out. Second Story created four installations throughout the Armory lobby: "Meet Portland Center Stage" interactive poster screens display information and videos about current PCS productions; "The Historiscope" invites visitors to peer into the past through the portals of a peep-show style cabinet revealing the history of the Armory from 1891 to the present day; "Saving the Past, Building the Future," an interactive exhibit, explores the value of preserving our architectural heritage and reveals the many sustainability-minded design features in the renovation that earned the Armory LEED Platinum rating for green building excellence and energy efficiency; and the "PCS Donor Wall" light sculpture recognizes the names of all those who have contributed to realizing this new chapter in PCS history. • Since I moved to Portland in 1997, the Armory was always close to the heart of where I lived and worked. For many years the unique fortress-like exterior of the building seemed to taunt the passersby as it both elicited wonder and eluded understanding. The very windows that inspired curiosity hid what was inside as it sat there, a kind of quiet, mysterious, gestating vessel amid the explosive growth that surrounded it. Now it has awakened — not merely to be restored or renovated, but to be transformed into a place that at once embraces its colorful past and becomes something entirely new. We are proud to live in a city that preserves and protects its heritage, and we are happy to help inspire, entertain and inform our community about this important landmark and Portland Center Stage through interactive media. Each new Center Stage production will continue to transform it again and again, and every time we go there, it will be something new for us.

Brad Johnson is the Co-Founder and Creative Director of Second Story Interactive Studios, a Portland-based interactive media studio that creates informative and entertaining websites, media and installations for many of the world's great museums and cultural institutions.

A 19TH-CENTURY PORTLAND ICON

Stalwart and Steady in All Its Permutations

Downtown Portland in 1891 was a different place. Main Street was First Avenue while the block east was filled with wharfs, docks and warehouses on the west bank of the Willamette. The city had just annexed East Portland and now had a population of 62,000 spread among 26 square miles. The leading building was the New Market Theater, built in the 1870s, which defined the social epicenter of town. • Ten blocks north was the National Guard First Regiment Armory. Across the street was the North Portland Public School and nearby the city's stables. The original Armory building, built in 1887, was a cavernous, castellated brick and basalt two-story battery and drill hall on a half-block parcel fronting on 10th Avenue. The roots of the First Regiment dated to the territorial days of Oregon when the government rallied volunteer armies to fight the natives. In 1887, the state legislature passed the "Summers Law," which authorized the formation of a permanent National Guard with three regimental districts. The First Regiment was based in Portland. The Second was in Salem, and the Third in the Columbia Valley. At the same session, Oregon House Bill No. 2 also authorized counties to erect "an armory, safe, suitable and of sufficient size for the drill of a company." Multnomah County acquired a full block bounded by North 10th and 11th, C and D Streets for $15,250. The county subsequently allocated $32,000 to build Portland's Armory. The architect was Irishman William F. McCaw, a leading Portland architect who also designed the Commanding Officer's Quarters at Fort Vancouver (1886), First Presbyterian Church (1889), University of Portland's West Hall (1891) and the Dekum Building (1892). The ceremonies opening Oregon's first Armory then were held in October, 1887. • Nearly upon completion, the First Regiment outgrew its original building and plans for an annex began. The architect for the annex was again McCaw. The addition completed the block, doubled the size of the Armory facilities and, constructed of the same brick and basalt as the original, continued the architectural designs of the original. The new hall featured a wood-truss roof system that provided a 100-foot north-south clear-span that not only allowed military drills but also concerts and even baseball games. Around the perimeter was a mezzanine gallery with space for audiences of 5,000. • The National Guard used the Armory for the next 80 years. In 1966, the Guard sold the building to the Blitz-Weinhard Brewing Company to raise money for a new facility. Blitz used the site for storage and in 1968 demolished the 1887 building, retaining the 1891 annex as a warehouse. When Blitz closed in the late 1990s, their five-block brewing complex was acquired by Gerding/Edlen Development Company.

An historian by training, John Tess is owner and president of Heritage Consulting Group. Founded in 1982, the firm works nationally to help owners and developers understand the historic character of their properties and devise viable strategies for reuse and redevelopment using federal, state and local historic preservation incentives. In 25 years, Heritage has represented historic projects totaling over $1 billion in construction.

THE AGORA AND THE THEATRON

A Play, a Public Forum

MEAD
HUNTER

Mead Hunter is the Director of Literary and Education Programs at Portland Center Stage.

Theater, as the ancient Greeks conceived of it, encompassed two broad categories. Tragedy was cathartic, intended for the purging of excess emotions from the human psyche. But comedy was a different matter altogether. Always topical and immediate, Greek comedies focused on contemporary society; they looked appraisingly and often satirically at its mores, politics and literature. Every citizen came to these events, from the magistrates to the plebeians, and regarded the comedies as dramatized public forums. • More than two millennia later, this critical purpose of comedy has come full circle. Thanks to the plethora of escapist fare readily available through other media, the stage has gladly surrendered the field, for the most part eschewing broad boulevard comedy in favor of more trenchant fare. But does this mean that modern theater is wholly serious? Hardly. Like the ancient Romans, today we believe that theater must be instructive and entertaining. • Of course only rarely, nowadays, do people come together in large numbers to bear witness to dramatized civic dialogues. For this purpose, many communities — Portland, for one — prefer smaller, more intimate settings, which allow audiences to sit close to stage action and to watch the play in close proximity to actors. Today's theatergoers want to see both the play itself and one another, to feel that they are engaged in a public forum together. • Equally complicit in this exchange are today's playwrights. Whereas some 60 years ago, writers tended to write "naturalistically," as though the audience eavesdropped on an actual, real-time conversation, now playwrights often conceive of their plays "presentationally"— that is, the characters are cognizant of you there in the house, sometimes even speaking directly to you. This shift is the most profound change to happen to mainstream theater in the post-war era and has greatly enhanced the awareness that a play is a community event, one in which the spectators participate no less actively than the actors. • The theaters of the newly restored Armory structure beautifully reflect this sensibility, which is both ancient and modern. Like an indoor *agora*, the intimate and flexible settings of the new theaters and their lobbies are intended to serve as civic spaces — that is to say, as centers of social interaction and as expressions of democratic life on a personal scale. • Our modern word "theater," when used to signify the physical structure that houses the audience, hearkens back to another ancient Greek term, *theatron*, which literally means "seeing-place." Yet then as now, the listening is at least as important as the seeing. Guest artists who work at Portland Center Stage — the actors especially — frequently comment on how attentive and engaged our Portland audiences are. As anyone who has stood up in front of a public forum can tell you, active listening is the predicate to true dialogue. So welcome to your new home. We designed it with you in mind.

GIVING PORTLAND CREATIVE CLASS

Diversity: The Mother of Invention

CARL
TALTON

As a person who's been involved with community and economic development initiatives in Portland for more than 30 years, I've watched the evolution of many of the ideas that are now driving economic and political thought in our community. A central dynamic in Portland's economic and cultural climate is the impact of creative services on economic development. The trend is eloquently described in the book *The Rise of the Creative Class* (Basic Books, 2002) by Richard Florida. • To the casual observer, the seemingly rapid rise of Portland's creative class has been somewhat surprising. In fact Portland has been attracting creative activity for more than 20 years. What I am pleased to see is that the creative industry is now getting the recognition and support necessary to make it an effective part of the strategy to support our economy. • It seems the biggest challenge we have today in locating the creative movement in the mainstream of our economy is understanding that creativity is about more than the arts and entertainment industry. Our ability to take the disciplined, tried-and-true methods we have come to rely upon, and marry them with the new, unexpected, out-of-the-box thinking, is what makes something innovative, and ultimately it's what adds value. I believe "mixing things up" is what will give us our competitive edge over the rest of the world. • Portland takes great pride in the diversity of its city and state. Whether it's the geographic diversity of our landscape or the mix of our urban, suburban and rural communities, we have come to see the importance of all of it. Within our own city, the old categories and groups are redistributing and coming up with unexpected and vibrant results. A swirl of communities, styles and disciplines — ethnic, economic, contemporary, traditional, dense, greenspace, industrial, commercial, and residential — are debunking stereotypes, creating stunning spaces and impressive city blocks, making new equations and energy. The key is we see them all as valuable. • My central message here is that the beginning of creativity is diversity. Creativity is the great equalizer that puts all communities and ideas in the game. Whether I'm sitting in the office of a high-tech firm in Hillsboro, a media agency in the Pearl, or in a granny-flat in North Portland, I am equally as likely to generate the next valuable concept that keeps Portland moving forward. If diversity is key, then we are all participants in the creative class economy, no matter what we do for a living. • The Armory will represent one of Portland's largest public investments in the growth and development of the creative sector. The building itself — its design and construction — is a perfect example of the new role creativity will play in areas that are not viewed as the "arts." (That it is home to a theater is the finishing touch.) Everything from the cutting-edge, energy-saving aspects to the "ship in a bottle" construction have required the developers to think beyond the traditional approach. The artful revitalization of the Armory has given it tremendous value and a singular cachet, making it a model for future projects across the country.

Carl Talton is the Executive Chair of the Portland Family of Funds Board. He has 30 years experience in community economic development and leadership in Oregon's energy industry. Talton served as PGE Vice President, Community / Business Development, and spent 25 years working for PacifiCorp in various management positions.

RASSLIN' AT THE ARMORY

A Portlander Reminisces

JOHN
TERRY

John Terry is a long-time Portland denizen and retired journalist whose career spanned 40 years at the *Salem Capital Journal* and *The Oregonian*. He writes the weekly "Oregon's Trails" history column for *The Oregonian*.

Some buildings have a meaning far beyond their primary purpose. Portland is rife with examples, some long-since relegated to memory. • We of a certain age can't help regarding the downtown Meier & Frank building as not just another store but, in its heyday, as the true heart of the city. Union Station is not just where Amtrak trains come and go but symbolic of an age when rails were the main road to almost anywhere. • The late Vaughn Street baseball park, rickety as it was, remains the epitome of that sport in the city, and no amount of spiffying up will ever let PGE Park, nee Multnomah (Civic) Stadium, replace it. The Portland Hotel, irreverently dispatched in 1952, stands in memory as the ultimate hostelry in the city. • The Portland Armory is such a place. Its ersatz medievalness resounded not just with the rhythm of combat boots and close-order drills, but with Portlanders brought together for events great and small, an arena equal to tasks much more varied than those for which it was inaugurated. • My first memory of the building is of Shrine Circuses during my family's first tenure in the city, 1948-51. A few years later the Armory played host to Portland State basketball games against the University of Portland. • But my most vivid memory is of a "sport," mainly because one need not attend in person to partake: Portland Wrestling. Don and Elton Owen wrestling. Tom Peterson knocking on your TV screen wrestling. Barney Keep wisecracking in the "crow's nest" wrestling. • The purists pronounced it "rasslin'." My father never failed to refer to it as "Grunt and Groan." I'm not talking about the behemoths who nowadays inflate themselves on prime-time television—obnoxious, loudmouths on anabolic steroids. I am talking about such local darlings as "Tough" Tony Bourne, "Dutch" Savage and "Gentleman" Ed Francis. Real people, often using their real names, with real human dimensions, more often than not tending to extra girth. • While the action sometimes got out of hand, the boys were kept mostly on the right side of morality by the Owen clan who, as far as I could tell, had enjoyed a monopoly on Oregon pro wrestling since such entertainments began. A regular highlight, in fact, was Don Owen, of a size more that of Mr. Peepers, ascending the ring to rebuke an offense with tightlipped outrage and tone reminiscent of an offended English nanny. • The Owens accommodated us common folk with prices not prohibitive. I don't remember the exact freight, but $2 strikes me as about right. That and maybe 25 cents for peanuts and a buck for beer was all you needed for an evening's enlightenment. • And though they now may be loath to fess up, there will be those applauding the building's reincarnation as legitimate theater who cannot help but relish the delicious memory, the decadent drama of attending rasslin' in person, or sneaking in a match or two late Saturday on Channel 12 after mom and dad went to bed.

ARCHITECTURAL VISIONS

ARMORY VOICES:
Design

GBD RENDERINGS

GBD
ARCHITECTS

CORRALLING THE ANGELS:

...ning up the Armory Stakeholders

RUMBLINGS

Through 2001 and 2002, the executive directors of the Oregon Ballet Theatre, Oregon Symphony, ...land Opera and Center Stage began meeting on a regular basis. To describe ourselves, we used ...acronym BODS (the "D" is for Drama — don't ask who made that decision), but I prefer the ...hemism Kirk Watson, the former mayor of Austin, liked to use for the symphony, opera and ...t: "those SOBs." After a few times together, it became clear that long-term facility issues ... critical for each of the BODS companies. In January of 2002, a grant of $200,000 was ...red from an anonymous donor to conduct a feasibility study on the subject.

... process was primarily driven by Tony Woodcock, then president of the symphony, and ...e the initial vision was of a "Lincoln Center West" with four performance spaces, I didn't ...ct much to come of it for PCS. Both the opera and symphony wanted better spaces, but ...ter" seemed to mean more "elegant" with sharper acoustics. When I asked James Canfield ...mer artistic director of Oregon Ballet Theatre) his thoughts about the effort, he said, ...n't happen in my lifetime." So it was hard to know how much energy to invest.

...estly, my hopes were for a space that was less grand and more authentic. We wanted per-...nance spaces that were human and intimate, and a lobby that felt more uniquely "Portland."

Rumblings *continued*

Portland is a quirky place. It is not by accident that there are no buildings over 30 stories high (so the beauty of the horizon remains unmarred), that there are more farmers' markets than almost any city in the country, that the nation's first bottle-recycling bill and first assisted-suicide bill started here. It was no accident that in 2006 Portland was named the "most sustainable city in America" by SustainLane. It is no accident that the world's largest independently-owned bookstore resides in the same city that has one of the best public library systems in the United States. To find a comparable public transportation system for a city Portland's size, you have to fly to Munich or Amsterdam.

The Portland "culture" has been developed by thousands of different individuals, through thousands of different decisions — but the theme is usually "how can we make the community more livable?" The personality of the city is obstinately understated. If you want skyscrapers and glamour — go to San Francisco or Dallas. In Portland, you are as likely to find the wealthiest citizen riding a bike to work

Rumblings *continued*

(yes, wearing a helmet), as you are to see him in a tux at the opera. So to say that something "feels Portland" to me means it is smart in a substantive, forward-thinking way; it's comfortable for the most granola-crunching and the most fancy-schmancy among us; and it celebrates the quirky, untidy mixture of all these colliding ideals.

So we knew we wanted a more "Portland-y" theater, but making our case to the public was challenging. When I mentioned the desire for a new space to the general public, people would ask, "What's wrong with the space you're in?" After all, the Newmark Theatre in the Portland Center for the Performing Arts is a very handsome performance space in a good location. Why complain?

What most people didn't stop to consider were the drawbacks of the original design for a modern regional theater company. There was no anchor tenant when the Newmark was first constructed; the designers had no clear direction on what the space would be used for. No one could decide if it should be a theater, an opera house, or a touring venue. So it landed somewhere in-between.

Take the size of the proscenium opening (48'wide, by 26' high). Not bad for a musical, or Shakespeare, but for anything that asks for a more human scale, that huge opening can eat the show alive. I vividly remember rehearsing *The Seagull*. After spending time in Hungary, Poland and

> Honestly, my hopes were for a space that was less grand and more authentic. We wanted performance spaces that were human and intimate, and a lobby that felt more uniquely "Portland." The personality of the city is obstinately understated...So in imagining a new home for PCS we wanted something intimate, human. Grand and elegant? Not so much.
>
> *Chris Coleman*

p54

Rumblings *continued*

Russia I was interested in unleashing the Slavic temperament inside Chekhov's soul.

American theater artists have never quite known what to do with Chekhov. The only late-19th-century social world we know well is England (think Shaw, Oscar Wilde). So we tend to think that Chekhov is writing about those people — just in a bigger country. But if you spend anytime in Eastern Europe or Russia, it becomes quickly evident that it is a different world altogether, with distinctive textures and relationships. An American journalist I met working in Moscow described Russian society as a "giant amoeba languidly galumphing its way through life." The kind of "Upstairs/Downstairs" stratification predominant in Victorian England never took hold in Russia — and households (even the wealthiest) tended to mash the servants and masters, relatives, lovers, and dogs all into one big pot. The Russian productions I saw captured this spirit in wildly divergent ways, but each intuitively understood the messy, earthy, emotional, smelly, sexy, musical, lazy, drunk, delicate world that

Chekhov was evoking. We Americans tend to be uncomfortable with "giant galumphing amoebas," so we try to tidy the productions up and make everyone more industrious than they are probably intended to be.

In rehearsal for our *Seagull*, the cast spent a fair amount of time improvising, and we hired two local Russian musicians to teach us folks songs, dances and a bit of the language. A deliciously spontaneous sense emerged in the piece, with actors wandering on and off the stage with casual abandon.

Then we moved into the theater. What had been a casual exit in the rehearsal hall suddenly became an eight-foot trek to the wings of the stage — giving it much more significance than it should have had. The size of the stage picture in the Newmark means that every physical gesture becomes a "STATEMENT" whether you want it to or not.

In Portland, you are as likely to find the wealthiest citizen riding a bike to work (yes, wearing a helmet), as you are to see him in a tux at the opera. So to say that something "feels Portland" to me means it is smart in a substantive, forward-thinking way; it's comfortable for the most granola-crunching and the most fancy-schmancy among us; and it celebrates the quirky, untidy mixture of all these colliding ideals.

Chris Coleman

So in imagining a new home for PCS we wanted something intimate, human, and authentic. Grand and elegant? Not so much.

In July 2002 the BODS leaders gathered to hear results of the feasibility study, and the cost analyst revealed that the Lincoln Center West model would cost $500 million.

IN JULY 2002, ARTS LEADERS GATHERED TO
HEAR RESULTS OF THE FEASIBILITY STUDY
AND THE COST ANALYST REVEALED THAT THE
"LINCOLN CENTER WEST" MODEL WOULD
COST $500 MILLION.

DEAD SILENCE. LONG PAUSE.
AND A FEW HEAVY SIGHS.

MORE SILENCE. FOLLOWED BY SQUIRMING.
AND A FEW HEAVY SIGHS.

AFTER A FEW MOMENTS, I SAID, "DOES ANYONE
IN THIS ROOM BELIEVE THERE IS $500 MILLION
IN OREGON FOR THIS PROJECT?" NO ONE DID.
Chris Coleman

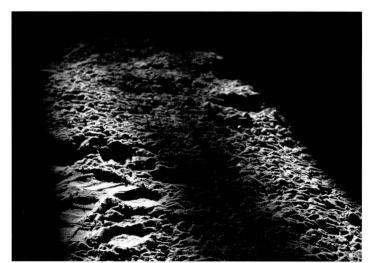

Dead silence. Long pause. And a few heavy sighs.

More silence. Followed by squirming. And a few heavy sighs.

After a few moments, I said, "Does anyone in this room believe there is $500 million in Oregon for this project?" No one did. So we went back to the drawing board.

After several months, the consultants (Keewaydin Group out of Minneapolis) came back with a series of steps to be phased in over a decade which were calibrated to the level of support the community seemed willing to consider. Their first recommendation was that PCS should move out of the Newmark and find or build a home of its own; thus freeing up space for possible performances by the ballet and opera; in turn loosening up the chronic logjam at the Keller Auditorium where they both performed.

Our move was the first step because at a price tag of $20 - $35 million it was the cheapest piece of the puzzle, and it was also probably the quickest to bring to fruition. Keewaydin also suggested that renovation of an existing building might suit the company's economic and aesthetic needs.

The study was published in mid-September of 2002, and within days, Bob Gerding called to say he wanted to talk about the Armory. Constructed in 1891, the Armory was situated in the heart of the Brewery Block development that Bob's company had brought to life and was owned by a small group of investors. The Pearl District, the immediate surrounding neighborhood, had become one of the most vibrant parts of the city, changing dramatically during my first two years in Portland. It had recently been named the "Outstanding Example of

Urban Neighborhood Design in North America" by
the Partnership for Public Spaces. With heavy pedestrian traffic, Whole Foods two blocks away, Powell's
Books (the city's most popular bookstore) one block
south, and the shiny new Portland Streetcar running
on both sides of the building, the location was an arts
manager's dream. Gerding/Edlen had talked to REI,
the outdoor supplies retailer, about putting a new store
into the Armory. But that hadn't quite worked. Several
other retailers sniffed around, but because it is a historic
building you can't put windows at street level on the exterior, making retail sales a very difficult proposition.
There were two other options on the table.

The first, and most serious, was to put a health club
into the building. In fact, architectural plans had been
drafted, and a preliminary lease drawn up to convert
the Armory into a gym. The other plan would demolish the Armory and build a new office building or
hotel on the site. The long process of obtaining demolition permits on a historic structure already had been
set in motion. Both could make economic sense for
the investors, but Bob wasn't satisfied with either one.

Rumblings *continued*

The Armory had such an amazing history, and though it had been empty for several years, the potential for its cultural and architectural rebirth was easy to imagine. The notion that such a strange and wonderful building would end up as a gym was just not a good enough community use in Bob's mind.

From the first time that Creon and I walked into the Armory, we had hinted to Bob that it would make a great theater. Sometimes he seemed interested; other times he wasn't sure. We had also talked about the Galleria (a retail center downtown where sales were sagging), the notion of rehabbing the Newmark (if we could buy the entire building), and constructing a theater from the ground up (perhaps on the East Side of the Willamette River, across from downtown). None got any real traction. Bob loved the idea of the Armory as a theater, but he hadn't yet figured out how to make it financially possible.

When it became clear that the alternatives for the building's future were so unsatisfactory, and

I'M A THEATER GUY. AS A BOY I LOVED STORIES —
HEMINGWAY, JACK LONDON, ASIMOV, BRADBURY.
I BECAME HOOKED ON THE LIFE OF THE MIND. I
WENT INTO THE ARMY AND WAS SENT TO EUROPE.
I MANAGED TO HOOK UP WITH A BUNCH OF GUYS
WHO WANTED TO EXPLORE THE CULTURE OF
EUROPE, SO WE SAW EVERY PERFORMANCE,
EVERY EXHIBITION, EVERY PAINTING AND SCULPTURE
WE COULD. AFTER THE WAR, I EARNED MY PH.D.
AS A BIOCHEMIST, BUT MY PASSION FOR CREATIVE
EXPRESSION NEVER STILLED. THEATER CAN BE JOYFUL,
ENTERTAINING AND ALSO DIFFICULT. IT'S A DEEPLY
EMOTIONAL CHALLENGE TO EXPERIENCE A PLAY LIKE
WIT AND LIVE THAT WOMAN'S JOURNEY THROUGH
CANCER, OR *CROWNS* AND GET A GLIMPSE OF THE
LIVES OF AFRICAN AMERICAN WOMEN. THESE ARE
NOT MY LIVES, BUT IN THE THEATER I GET TO LIVE THEM
FOR A FEW HOURS, AND FEEL THEIR JOY AND PAIN.
THEATER IS ONE OF THE LAST PLACES WHERE THE
COMMUNITY GATHERS AROUND THE FIRE TO SHARE
THE GREAT ARCHETYPAL STORIES, THE EXPOSITION
OF THE GREAT TRUTHS THAT WE SHARE AS HUMANS
IN ALL THEIR BEAUTY AND UGLINESS AND LYRICISM
AND MUSIC. IT'S A CHALLENGE I WELCOME AND
EMBRACE AND WANT TO SHARE.

Bob Gerding. Principal,
Gerding/Edlen Development

Rumblings *continued*

after he read the BODS study, Bob asked if we thought the Armory could actually work as a theater and we answered emphatically, "Yes!" Why did Bob get it at this moment? Two reasons, I believe. He understood that PCS's real chance at a future was linked to creating the right home, and that this was perhaps the most viable option for making that happen.

I also believe Bob felt strongly that the Brewery Blocks development would be fine if a gym went into the building, but that it could be *AMAZING* if the city's largest theater moved in. His original idea behind the Brewery Blocks was that, if successful, it could transform the city. The prospect of that transformation occurring only increased with Portland Center Stage at the heart of the development.

So Bob jumped into our first discussion of a financing structure that would corral a group of "angels" to buy the building in exchange for use of the historic tax credits, for which the Armory qualified. I tried my darnedest to keep up with the conversation, but after about half an hour I had no idea what he was talking about. What was clear, though, was that he was serious about converting the Armory into a theater for Portland Center Stage.

> To me, the Armory project is a rebirth of public place. This space was a near fortress, emanating exclusion and alienation. The Armory project turns this past inside out, toward a vision of inclusion and inspiration. Seeing a welder at work seemed a perfect symbol of this transformation, fusing history to future, illuminating the dark with sparks of imagination. I am honored to help bring the joy of such imagination to every Portlander through projects that, like the Armory, invite every community to come, to remember, and to create anew together."
> *Sam Adams,* City Commissioner and former Chief of Staff for Mayor Vera Katz

The stars were beginning to align.

Rumblings *continued*

In early October, I had lunch with Sam Adams (then Mayor Vera Katz's chief of staff, now a city commissioner). Sam and I had become gym buddies during the first summer I arrived in Portland, and as a political junkie I loved hearing about the wheelings and dealings of his career. Though our lunch was officially a catch-up meeting, I also sounded Sam out about prospects for a third installment of operating support from the city. He was not encouraging, given the amount of money they were trying to cut from the budget, but he asked what else was going on, and I mentioned the Armory.

Now, good student that he is, Sam had already read the BODS report and had also begun to study Richard Florida's book, *The Rise of the Creative Class* — which identifies the link between a city's creative energy and its economic competitiveness. He had encouraged his boss to read both items, and together they were looking for a way to take some initiative in this area. Sam suggested that Vera might be interested in p68

Rumblings *continued*

helping connect us to the Portland Development Commission. He knew she loved the Armory, because she walked past it on her way to work, and he agreed to discuss the idea with her.

SHIP IN A BOTTLE

Meanwhile, Bob arranged for Creon and me to meet with a designer from GBD Architects (the designers of the Brewery Blocks) to draft initial plans for a theater. GBD's offices are in the converted Weinhard Brewery on Northwest Couch Street, a gorgeous juxtaposition of historic brick textures set against sleek, clean contemporary finishes. Renderings of the South Waterfront, future Pearl District buildings, and projects up and down the West Coast line the walls.

Our task was to put our space needs on paper so that an expert could determine whether the plans could work in the existing building. GBD's Steve Domreis, helped sort through the ideas in our heads. I imagined a mainstage of 500-535 seats,

Ship in a Bottle *continued*

and a studio theater with 150-200 seats. For a while we considered two theaters that were both 350 seats (modeling the successful solution at the Studio Theatre in Washington, D.C.) but then realized that the opportunity to produce works of scale would be harder to pay for in those spaces. Given our commitment to maintaining salaries that can attract a high caliber of actor, if a show requires a cast of more than 16, it becomes almost impossible to break even in a house with fewer than 500 seats. Knowing we wanted to keep producing musicals, and large-scale dramas, 599 seats became the answer.

We also knew we wanted rehearsal space, administrative offices, a costume shop, dressing rooms, and perhaps classrooms in the building. We liked the idea of making the lobby space active with events throughout the week. We weren't sure what the programming would be, but the notion of collaborating with Powell's Books on an author reading series had been mentioned, as had book groups, music performances, and tai chi classes (yes, tai chi classes). How it would all fit into the building, we had no clue.

Steve drew plans that apportioned the space into various configurations. (We initially thought the studio theater would live above the lobby). Bob brought in Hugh Hardy, the country's most respected renovator of performance spaces, to look at the building. Hugh believed we could fit the desired "program" (architect-speak for the arrangement of spaces) into the building, but we would have to cut through the roof in order to create "fly space" (the area that allows you to drop scenery from above) for the mainstage theater. Bob explained that due to the historic nature of the structure, that wouldn't be possible; Hugh countered that we would then have to excavate.

Bob thought for a moment, sighed and replied, "That's going to be very expensive."

p72

THE ARMORY RECLAIMS VITALITY

Banking on Community-Building Cachet

As part of the fabric of Portland's Pearl District, the Armory building blazes a trail for historic projects looking to contribute to the economic vitality of once-neglected neighborhoods. • The $36 million retrofit, rehabilitation and redesign of the 19th-century landmark is a small part of the transformation and revitalization of the city's booming Pearl District, but it is a principal player nationally as one of the earliest and largest projects in the country to combine federal New Markets Tax Credits with historic tax credits. When the arts center opens in the fall of 2006 as the permanent home for Portland Center Stage, the federal tax credits will have played a central role in providing the community with two theaters, administrative offices, an interactive public lobby, a costume shop, rehearsal hall and other theater-related facilities. • Created by legislative mandate in December 2000, the New Markets Tax Credits (NMTC) program encourages new, private sector investments in, and delivers new resources and benefits to, underserved communities. Under the NMTC program, community development entities will use $5.85 billion in tax credits to raise $15 billion in capital to invest in low-income communities. NMTCs are claimed over seven years and used by community development entities to raise more patient investor capital. The NMTC program is administered by the Community Development Financial Institutions Fund. The last congressionally authorized NMTC funding round is expected to occur in the fall of 2006. There is currently an effort in Congress to authorize additional funding rounds. • The Federal Historic Preservation Tax Incentive Program was enacted in 1976 to encourage private developers and investors to restore historic buildings to productive use. Under the historic tax credit program, owners of historic buildings are eligible for a 20% tax credit for qualified rehabilitation costs. In order to qualify for the credits, however, the rehabilitation has to be certified by the National Park Service (within the Department of Interior). In evaluating a rehabilitation for certification, the National Park Service reviews whether the work was done in a manner that retained the historic fabric of the building. • To obtain the level of NMTC financing needed, the Armory project reached out to Goldman Sachs and the Historic Rehabilitation Fund to raise about $36 million in NMTC subsidized equity. Also critical to the overall project financing was a capital campaign by the project's chief tenant, Portland Center Stage. • The combination of historic and NMTC credits supported the performing arts center in a way that conventional financing alone could not. By combining tax credits with traditional capital, the Armory's developers created an exceptional project that added to the Pearl District's growing prominence, helped stimulate the local economy, generated new jobs and, perhaps most importantly, acted as a catalyst for similar tax credit projects across the country.

MICHAEL J. NOVOGRADAC

Michael J. Novogradac, CPA, is the managing partner in the San Francisco office of Novogradac & Company LLP. He specializes in real-estate taxation and syndication, and is the author of numerous articles on real-estate topics, including the *New Markets Tax Credit Handbook* and the *Low-Income Housing Tax Credit Handbook*.

THE ARMORY AND THE MAN

Biochemist, Developer, Theater Guy

BOB GERDING

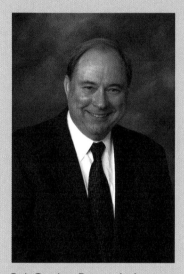

Bob Gerding, Principal of Gerding/Edlen Development Company, LLC, has been active in the Portland commercial real estate market for more than 20 years. Gerding/Edlen projects include the Brewery Blocks in the Pearl District, Bank of America, Collins Circle Apartments, Floyd Light Apartments, the South Waterfront, and the Wieden & Kennedy building.

Three years ago, we had a lease in hand from a company that wanted to develop a fitness center in the Armory. As the last piece of the Brewery Blocks, it would have been a pretty good fit. We also knew that the city had been interested in developing another idea, a new theater and home for Portland Center Stage, which had received a recommendation from a national theater consultant to move from its space in downtown. Due to several considerations at the time, a decision was looming. • As a business, we've been successful in making the " Brewery Blocks" a great destination that built on the presence and success of Powell's Books, the Wieden + Kennedy headquarters, Blue Hour restaurant, and the rest of the Pearl District. In the five Brewery Blocks, we preserved the historically significant buildings and facades of the original buildings, and used the rest of the land to build a complex, dense neighborhood where pedestrians thrive, retailers are exceeding all expectations, and office space is near capacity. The last piece, the star in the crown so to speak, was the Armory. • The decision was difficult on some levels, but ultimately, the deciding factor was singular. What would be best for the city and the Pearl District? I was told as a young man, and have really come to believe, that you are not what you say. You are how you act. You are what you do. And you are what you leave behind. At the critical moment, the call came from the city — they were ready to go. And so were we — with the theater. • Then again, I'm a theater guy. As a boy I loved stories — Hemingway, Jack London, Asimov, Bradbury. I became hooked on the life of the mind. I was fortunate to have such teachers as Mrs. Arbuckle at Lincoln High School, who opened my eyes to the potential of great stories and language to stimulate my imagination. When I got to the University of Oregon, I was lucky again to study under a professor named Jake Straus, who sealed the deal for me. Soon after, I went into the Army and was sent to Europe. I managed to hook up with a bunch of guys who wanted to explore the culture of Europe, so we saw every performance, every exhibition, every painting and sculpture we could. After the war, I earned my Ph.D. as a biochemist, but my passion for creative expression never stilled. My wife and I joined friends for regular trips to Ashland and the Oregon Shakespeare Festival, and I joined the board of Portland Center Stage to help bring that experience to others in Portland. • Theater can be joyful, entertaining and also difficult. Sometimes it's hard to watch the truth unfold before your eyes, especially when you're in the room and can't look away. It's a deeply emotional challenge to experience a play like *Wit* and live that woman's journey through cancer, or *Crowns* and get a glimpse of the lives of African American women. These are not my lives, but in the theater I get to live them for a few hours, and feel their joy and pain. Theater is one of the last places where the community gathers around the fire to share the great archetypal stories, the exposition of the truths that we share as humans in all their beauty and ugliness and lyricism and music. It's a challenge I welcome and embrace and want to share. • All the hard work, hard decisions, and paths not taken were all a means to this end. We made sacrifices to get the theater done at the Armory, and I laud the partnership of Mark Edlen and his effervescent commitment to the community. The theater was the right choice — anything else would just have been done to make money, but wouldn't have meant as much to the fabric of Portland. • The Armory project isn't finished when the doors open. The relationship between the theater and the audience will be just beginning. When they connect, we as a city, as a community, will be better for it.

FROZEN MUSIC ON AN OLD SCORE

GBD Designs Inside the Box

ALAN BEARD

There must be a thousand easier ways to build a theater. • There's no question that the Portland Armory project has provided GBD Architects with some of the biggest challenges in our 37 years as a firm. It's been a fascinating project because there was no road map to follow (and perhaps there's a lesson here) to create 55,000 square feet of space inside a 20,000 square foot building; to stack two theaters inside an existing historic building; to install a new foundation and seismic bracing in a building that's attached to an inhabited condominium, all while being designed to LEED Platinum Sustainability standards — a first for a building on the National Register of Historic Places. • To accomplish all this, we were challenged to address the desires and requirements of numerous masters — The US Green Building Council; the State Office of Historic Preservation; the developer; the engineers; the sustainable designers; the interior designers; the community; sound engineers; theater designers; landscape architects, and by the way, the client, Portland Center Stage — all of whom sometimes had conflicting requirements. We were fortunate to work with many deeply talented and committed professionals, almost all from the local area, whose expertise and work ethic inspired us. • Preserving historic buildings means a lot to us as individuals, as residents of this city, and as professional architects. It was important to showcase the Armory's parallel-chord wooden barrel trusses, turrets and arched doorways (now there are two arches again, as when the building was constructed in 1891), the Columbia River basalt foundation and the original windows with their sandstone sills. • No one will ever see the hundreds of small design decisions, meetings, about-faces, material and measurement reconfigurations that created the end result. They will see the conscious decisions to use as little finish as possible so that the character of this great building can shine through for another century. • Truth is, there *are* a thousand easier ways to build a theater. We should know. We considered them all on any one aspect of the project. But the Armory demanded new solutions to new challenges almost every step of the way.

Alan Beard is a Principal at GBD Architects, a Portland architectural firm with experience in mixed-use, housing, office-space, interior, space planning, retail, institutional and athletic design. GBD's mixed-use projects include the Brewery Blocks, the Belmont Dairy, Museum Place and South Waterfront.

ON VERA KATZ

A Mayor's Vision

MEL
KATZ

Vera Katz was elected the 45th mayor of Portland in 1992 and served three terms, leaving office in 2005. Mel Katz, a Portland sculptor, is Vera's former husband and long-time close friend.

Without passion, there cannot be great art, and without great art, there cannot be a great city. How lucky for Portland that art brought Vera Katz and her passion for protecting the city's artistic soul to us. A former dancer who studied under Martha Graham, Vera has always been buoyed by the arts, and she in turn lifted the arts community when it needed help. During her 20-year tenure in the Oregon Legislature, she was a sponsor of Oregon's Percent for Art Program. As Mayor, she secured special and substantial appropriations for the Portland Opera, Portland Art Museum, Oregon Ballet Theatre (OBT), and Oregon Symphony. She pushed for neighborhoods to have direct access to the arts via OBT Exposed (free, outdoor dance rehearsals in Portland's South Park Blocks) and Symphony in the Parks. She initiated a new design festival and garnered special support for Portland Institute for Contemporary Art's

TBA Festival. Vera did all this because she understood that imagination is the bridge between inspiration and action, and that as Jane Jacobs (1916-2006) wrote in her 1961 book *The Death and Life of Great American Cities*, "Designing a dream city is easy. Rebuilding a living one takes imagination." "Over time, a city can deteriorate or continue to improve. But it can never stand still," Vera said in her 1998 State of the City address. Vera recognized this did not mean "out with the old and in with the new," but that preserving the architectural heritage of a city could be an act of regeneration. And so she embraced the saving of the Armory and encouraged the marriage of the arts and preservation. Vera encouraged the Portland Development Commission (PDC), the city's economic development and urban renewal agency, to help the Armory become one of the first recipients of an innovative new federal financing program called New Markets Tax Credits. Working with the Portland Family of Funds, an early recipient of a New Markets allocation and local expert on the tax credit program, PDC was able to assist the project in obtaining credits from Goldman Sachs that provided essential gap financing for the project. It was a model of the types of pioneering public private partnerships that prospered during Vera's term as mayor. In her address at the closing of the Armory transaction in April, 2004, Katz ended by saying: "The Armory is a bridge between the past and the future. Between the arts and the economy, sustainability and the community. And when it's finished, the Armory will be a bridge between Portland and the world. Thanks to all of you for bringing this bridge to our community."

A STRUCTURAL PERSPECTIVE

Gaining Ground on a Wish

BLAKE PATSY

Working in the Pearl District, I walked by the old Armory building countless times hoping that one day I would be the structural engineer of record for its next incarnation. A wise person once said, "Be careful what you wish for." The structural renovation of the Armory presented several significant challenges. • The installation of a new below-grade theater and ancillary spaces required a 30-foot-plus excavation next to The Henry, a 15-story retail and condominium high-rise, which is founded on a shallow, continuous raft foundation (there is no basement). Any disruption of the ground next to it can compromise the Henry's structural integrity, a possibility that led the design team to several sleepless nights. Imagine placing a hole next to the foundation of a brand-new, elite condominium tower the occupants of which include the project developer, Bob Gerding, the man for whom the theater is named. • Engineering for the shoring was difficult not only because of the magnitude of the building surcharge (surcharge is the load that needs to be resisted by the shoring so that the Henry does not settle) but also because of the space constraints that we would soon realize were an over-riding theme for the remainder of the project. In order to save space and construction dollars, we ended up utilizing temporary, steel-pile shoring as part of the permanent basement wall and foundations for the Armory. • The 1891 Armory building had to be strengthened to meet the current seismic requirements of the 2003 International Building Code (IBC). To stabilize and strengthen the building, the new theater "box" was built inside the existing Armory walls. Obtaining city approval on one key building-code appeal (to satisfy a new requirement for the old, unreinforced masonry walls) allowed us to use the old brick walls without the addition of a layer of concrete or other materials that would be costly and cover the historic brick finish. Connecting the old unreinforced walls to the new structure made obtaining this approval easier. Once the "box" is tied into the old building, the two act together to meet the code requirements. • Due to the size of the existing Armory, every new element that was placed inside the building was carefully coordinated to make sure it took up no more space than absolutely required. This allowed the client, Portland Center Stage, to obtain as much program space as possible.

Blake D. Patsy, PE, SE, is a Principal/Structural Engineering Manager at KPFF Consulting Engineers in Portland. He serves as a principal-in-charge for seismic renovation projects or as a primary contact for KPFF during schematic design.

CH:3 BUILDING STEAM:
The Art of Finance and Design

LAUNCHING THE PLAN On the political front, Sam Adams had arranged for Bob, Julie and me to meet with the mayor to discuss the project, and Vera agreed to kindle the Portland Development Commission's (PDC) interest. Bob's group of "angels" had not materialized, and we were hoping to convince PDC to buy the building and take it off the market so we'd have time to conduct a capital campaign. With the newly completed condo towers in the Pearl District and Brewery Blocks selling out in days, the Armory was sitting on the hottest piece of real estate in Oregon, and the possibility that Bob would be able to stave off investors indefinitely was remote.

Initial conversations with PDC were difficult. Our project was not a natural fit for the commission, which traditionally reinvests Tax Increment Financing (TIF) dollars into projects in Urban Renewal Areas. It took persistence and creativity to see if a relationship could work. Had it not been for Sam Adams's understanding of the vision, and his doggedness in moving it forward, the project might have collapsed at this stage.

In March 2003, Julie Vigeland (who was still PCS board chair, and our most active fund-raiser) and I appeared before the Commission to make our case. It was an endless meeting, with developers and neighborhood leaders packed into the room and impatiently waiting their turn to be

Launching *continued*

heard. I was extremely nervous and kept thinking, "What in the world am I doing here?" Back in grad school when I dreamed about running a theater, I never once saw a hearing before the Portland Development Commission in my future.

The commissioners expressed varying degrees of interest in the project but seemed antsy about allocating TIF dollars for the deal. I believe it was Janis Wilson, perhaps the most vocal opponent, who said, "I am not comfortable using public dollars to buy out a private investor's building." This was completely new territory for me. At the time, I didn't even know what TIF dollars were, let alone why you would be uncomfortable using them for this purpose. To my mind, it was a great project for the community, and if you could help get it off the ground, why wouldn't you do that? Chicago had just allocated $18.8 million to help the Goodman build a new theater, the Minnesota legislature had ponied up $25 million for the new Guthrie Theater, and the city of Las Vegas was about to

Launching *continued*

chip in $100 million for a new performing arts center. $3 million to get this project off the ground didn't seem such a huge investment.

One slim ray of hope emerged from the hearing. The chair of the commission directed staff of the new "Resource Development Department" to see if there were alternative means of seeding the project. Still, it felt like we were being graciously blown off.

Walking up SW 18th Avenue to my house that night, I was totally depressed. We had been working hard on this thing, and it seemed so close. Now it was looking like we would be stuck in the Newmark for the rest of eternity. It was March, but unusually warm out, one of those aberrant bursts of decent weather during the Portland winter that trick you into thinking spring has arrived. I stopped in the middle of the street to call Julie.

OK, when you first meet Julie Vigeland you think she is probably a wonderful hostess. She is full of enthusiasm and warmth. You can imagine civilized dinners in her comfortable home overlooking the city, with rich, intelligent conversation coursing through the evening. And you would not be disappointed. She dresses impeccably, is always on time, and has the stamina of the Energizer Bunny (due in no small part to hours in the pool, where she trained to become a national champion synchronized swimmer). But after you've known Julie for a while, you also learn that the woman has a spine of steel.

She picked up the other line and I said: "What do you think? Is it time to chuck it? Should we just give up on this thing?"

Launching *continued*

She thought for several moments. Then said: "Chris. I know you and me well enough by now to know that we won't be able to give it up. We have to try. We have to pursue the route they've opened and see how far we can take it."

So on we went, not really knowing if we would find the funds to achieve lift-off. The design process lurched forward in fits and starts. Creon was our point man on the project by now, and he consistently provided exactly what you want in the job: deep knowledge of construction, interest in the details, a focused ear, and a complete inability to be ruffled. We began research with our counterparts around the country. Berkeley Repertory Theatre, San Jose Repertory Theatre, Playwrights Horizons, South Coast Repertory and Dallas Theater Center all had either recently built theaters or were soon to enter construction. They were invaluable in helping us know what to expect from design firms, in offering information about costs, and in showing us how to structure

Launching *continued*

a capital campaign. Creon gathered critical data from GeVa Theatre in Rochester, NY, a company that had renovated an Armory building almost the same size as ours. We compared operating costs and began to understand how much it would take to run the plant if we ever got it built.

Conversations with various theater designers helped define our vision for the performance spaces. When you ask a designer to dream about a space as exciting as the Armory, the designer tends to go crazy and draw the fanciest theater imaginable. Which could be fun. But my priority was making certain that audience members could have a great experience in the theaters. I had been in "super cool" spaces that had crappy acoustics or bizarre sightlines, so I was more inclined toward simplicity.

Each firm asked about my favorite theaters in the world, and I narrowed the list to four:

> Professional companies know what they want and Center Stage wanted less formality and a recessive space that would disappear when the house lights went down. As a theater group that does not focus on any one specific era or style, it needed a performance venue that didn't call attention to itself. In this context, the requirement is not for a great and original form-giver, but for an understanding that the production rather than the architecture is the star of the show.
>
> *Landry & Bogan,* Theater Designers

1) The Munich Kamerspiele: 250 seats, a small balcony; the stage is about 40 feet wide, and 100 feet deep. You can produce *Aida* on that stage, but the house is so intimate that an actor's voice is clear throughout;

2) The Majestic at the Brooklyn Academy of Music: at 800 seats, it's larger than I like, but the raw quality of the interior offers a wonderful tactile experience of the building's history;

THE ARMORY PROJECT HAS BEEN AN
ADVENTURE IN COLLABORATION. THOUSANDS
OF PEOPLE INSIDE AND OUTSIDE PORTLAND
HAVE TOUCHED AND SHAPED THIS PROJECT IN
ONE WAY OR ANOTHER. THE IMMEDIATE RESULT
IS AN INSPIRING, ADAPTIVE REUSE OF AN ICONIC
HISTORIC PORTLAND BUILDING. THE LASTING
RESULTS WILL BE DEFINED BY THE HUNDREDS
OF THOUSANDS OF VISITORS WHO EXPERIENCE
THE BUILDING'S NEW LIFE AND THE THEATER
THAT IS CREATED WITHIN.

Colin M. Rowan. Transaction Manager,
Portland Family of Funds

3) New York Theatre Workshop: 150 seat off-Broadway house, with a nice-sized stage and brick walls on either side; it's a simple room that doesn't compete with the performance, but offers enough volume to do big work;

4) The Angus Bowmer Theatre in Ashland at the Oregon Shakespeare Festival: 600 seats, with a wonderful fan-shaped house, and a great relationship between actor and audience. There is something very accessible about that room.

After many discussions, we landed at Landry & Bogan, the San Francisco-based firm that designed the Bowmer and the New Theatre at Ashland, as well as La Jolla Playhouse, the Old Globe and Seattle Children's Theatre.

DIGGING IN

Our first meeting with PDC's Resource Development Department took place on April 1, 2003. Norris Lozano, the newly appointed head of the department, strode in, both guns a-blazing and got right down to business. A Texan of Mexican ancestry, Norris is a fast-thinking, fast-talking, former real-estate attorney and commercial developer. I felt at home with his energy, having word-processed for real-estate attorneys during my early days at Actor's Express. But keeping up with the guy was a challenge.

Julie and I laid out our ideas about the Armory and talked about what we thought it would take to pull it off. I believe that our first, pre-cost consultant estimate was in the neighborhood of $21 million. Norris then began discussing "New Markets Tax Credits"(NMTC), which sounded to me like something to do with grocery stores. He explained that the tax credits were a tool allocated by the US Treasury to bring catalytic dollars into targeted census tracts. At first blush, he felt the Armory Project might qualify.

Digging In *continued*

He also said that it could qualify for Historic Tax Credits and that his staff could assist us in applying for both. Having prepared many a grant proposal through the years, I imagined a two-page project description, and a one-page budget. Nothing in my experience prepared me for the exhaustive and Byzantine application process that would extend over months and months and months — and which would eventually lead to the Armory's innovative financing structure (see diagram on page 182).

Norris and his staff were tireless in helping guide us through the process, which required enormous due diligence. We had to flesh out every aspect of the project, including a 15-year operating pro forma that could withstand the scrutiny of potential investors.

As a small aside, I would note that my training is as an actor and director. As artistic director of a small theater company, I did draft the budgets for the first seven years of operation, but anyone who works with me will tell you that understanding the complexities of finance is not my strongest suit. At this

Digging In *continued*

time, PCS had been without a managing director for almost a year, (Mark Crawford had departed for Seattle in August, and we were in search mode), and I was trying like heck to track the intricacies of the project. I did have great support from senior staff and Greg Ness (our board finance chair), but early on I was the contact from meeting to meeting. To say that I was drinking from a fire hose would be no exaggeration.

Several months passed before I began to understand the New Markets and Historic tax credit ideas and why we would qualify for them. Initially I thought Norris was being optimistic, but after some research of my own, I began to see he might be right.

New Markets Tax Credits began as an idea of former President Bill Clinton when he was Governor of Arkansas, to give private investors an incentive to invest in areas they might not otherwise. Later formalized at the Federal level by the US Treasury, the program basically offers a "credit" against their tax bill to private entities (usually large corporations), which then invest

ANYONE WHO WORKS WITH ME WILL TELL YOU THAT UNDERSTANDING
THE COMPLEXITIES OF FINANCE IS NOT MY STRONGEST SUIT...I WAS
TRYING LIKE HECK TO TRACK THE INTRICACIES OF THE PROJECT...TO SAY
THAT I WAS DRINKING FROM A FIRE HOSE WOULD BE NO EXAGGERATION.
Chris Coleman

Digging In *continued*

cash into a project. It was a new program, difficult to translate into plain language, and that has sometimes resulted in controversy in communities where the credits have been allocated.

Norris and his team, through the formation of a private entity called Portland New Markets Fund, had tried to attract these dollars to Portland by applying for the tax credits to be used on a number of Portland projects and were waiting to hear if they received an allocation. The qualifying requirements were stringent, but Norris knew that the Armory fell into a qualifying census tract (as designated by the Feds); that the tax credits would allow the Armory Project to be built for around half the additional private dollars that might ordinarily be required; that NMTCs had been used to convert similar buildings into arts venues; and that PDC's leadership could likely make a strong case for success. He also felt that to get PDC support to move the deal forward, we would have to raise a substantial chunk of change up front.

So Julie and I started trying to figure out how to do that. In May we attended a seminar about capital campaigns, hosted by the MJ Murdock Charitable Trust. Toward the end of the two days, the consultant leading the workshop made a list of seven reasons NOT to do a capital campaign, spotlighting the major pitfalls encountered by nonprofits (the only one I remember said: "Don't partner with the government!"). Julie and I just looked at each other and burst out laughing. We didn't have all seven, but I think we had five.

> In May we attended a seminar about capital campaigns. Toward the end of the two days, the consultant leading the workshop made a list of seven reasons NOT to do a capital campaign, spotlighting the major pitfalls encountered by nonprofits (the only one I remember said: "Don't partner with the government!"). We didn't have all seven, but I think we had five.
>
> *Chris Coleman*

The next week, we asked George Thorn, our strategic planning guide and a veteran of several capital campaigns, for his assessment, to which he replied: "Look, you know that you need this building to succeed in the long-term, right? And you know that an opportunity like converting a historic building in the hottest retail location in a city, with heavy pedestrian traffic on all sides doesn't fall into your lap every day, right? And you know that THIS particular building is helping you qualify for tax credits that could make the project more cost-effective, right? So you're going to build a theater. Go raise a bunch of money."

We also met with Barbara Mahoney, former vice president of Willamette University, and development director for Oregon Health & Science University, who suggested that if our campaign was $21 million, then the lead gift should be $10 million. We about choked on our lunch. The largest gift PCS had ever received from an individual was $100,000.

Within the month, Julie and I had set a meeting with a gentlemen who'd recently come into a windfall. On the way to work that morning I remember thinking, "I'm going to ask someone for $5 million today. I'm going to ask someone for $5 million today." It was bizarre and funny at the same time. After our impassioned and eloquent description of how the Armory Project could change the world, that first request landed on rocky soil, as the gentleman replied, "I think it's an ugly building. Why don't they just tear it down?"

"Within the month Julie and I had set a meeting with a gentleman who'd recently come into a windfall. After our impassioned and eloquent description of how the Armory Project could change the world, that first request [for financial support] landed on rocky soil, as the gentleman replied, "I think it's an ugly building. Why don't they just tear it down?""

Chris Coleman

Digging In *continued*

As our meetings with Norris and his staff continued, the philosophical scope of the project began to
expand. Building a new theater was a great thing for
me and for our audience, but the selling point for
the NMTCs would be the Armory's potential for
larger impact in the community. Norris began
asking how the building could enhance the city's
leadership efforts in sustainability.

During the past three decades, Portland has
become one of the world's leaders in sustainable
building and design. Beginning with Governor
Tom McCall's landmark "Bottle Bill" in 1971,
requiring that all alcoholic and carbonated containers be recyclable, the state began thinking
about ways to preserve the natural beauty of the
environment. Oregon's leading edge land-use
legislation in the 1970s led to higher density
growth in cities. Portland's mayor at the time,
Neil Goldschmidt, championed revitalizing the
city's core and helped to create a public transportation system that dramatically reduced
dependence on cars.

Digging In *continued*

Through the 1980s "building green" seemed a heroic and vaguely romantic notion, but by 2003, the case had been made that building green was not only the right thing to do for the city, it was really smart business. With energy prices continuing to skyrocket, developers and architects who focused on sustainable design were watching their profitability grow exponentially. With more LEED (Leadership in Energy and Environmental Design) standard buildings per capita than any city in the United States, Portland had undeniably become a leader in this area. To insiders and environmental activists, the value of this success was transparent. To the average guy on the street (which on this topic, would include me) the buzzwords didn't necessarily translate into a clear narrative.

So as PCS began talking to the city about restoring the Armory, the question arose: could this building in some way help tell Portland's sustainability story? And, could the building, in fact, become the most spectacular example of sustainable design in the Northwest?

> Norris was very keen on the "sustainability showcase" idea, but I kept seeing images of salmon runs in the lobby. I remember saying, "I don't want someone walking into the building five years from now to see a play, and say, "What the heck is all this environmental stuff doing here?"
>
> *Norris Lozano*

I was clueless about what building a new theater had to do with anything green. I mean I figured I was doing my part for the environment by walking to work, and frankly I was a lazy recycler. Norris was very keen on the "sustainability showcase" idea, but I kept seeing images of salmon runs in the lobby. I remember saying, "I don't want someone walking into the building five years from now to see a play, and say, "What the heck is all this environmental stuff doing here?"

Digging In *continued*

But Norris understood the psychology of Portland better than I did. And he sensed that while there would be one level of aid for a new theater, if we were able to do something bold on the sustainability front as well, our chances of building support increased dramatically. I was all for making our case stronger, but I was also focused on staying true to our theater's mission. There were several extended and heated discussions during which Norris and I yelled at each other a lot. But as we have come to affectionately acknowledge, we are both aggressive Southerners, so a good boxing match now and then just means you're getting warmed up.

July 2003 was an insanely busy month. We were working on four new plays at JAW/West, including Glen Berger's *O Lovely Glowworm* (which I didn't understand, but found quite funny). Kate Robin, one of the writers from *Six Feet Under* was with us for the festival working on her play *Anon*, and I had the pleasure of directing Joe Fisher's homage to the ghosts of Mount St. Helens, called *Thunderbird*.

JAW (as we had come to call it) was always a respite in

Digging In *continued*

the year for me. A ten-day period when I was so busy artistically, that the other business of the theater had to fade into the background. The whole festival is designed as a total immersion for the writer and actors, as they wrestle intensely with the problems (and assets) of a new script and then throw a sketch of how it might feel up onto the stage. The process offers the author (who may have spent months or years only imagining the piece in front of a computer) a sense of what the audience's response might be, what is working and what isn't.

Kate's play dealt very bluntly with male infidelity and the objectification of women. And it was quite interesting to see audience responses split along generational lines about which of the characters were or were not sympathetic.

Thunderbird followed a fire jumper (fire fighters who parachute down into forest fires to put them out) as he confronts the traumatic loss of his girlfriend. Set on Mount St. Helens, with the ghosts of the 1981 eruption surfacing through the course of the story, I loved its resonance with the Northwest.

Digging In *continued*

And *Glowworm* was a whimsical/meditational farce about the meaning of life as imagined through the sufferings and fantasies of a stuffed goat. The rehearsal process was pretty tense as our lead actor and the director clashed about how sentimental or theatrical the playing of said "goat" should be, but the performance was sidesplitting and a clear audience favorite.

During the same period, we were interviewing finalists for the managing director job. Edith Love, whom I had known from her days as managing director of the Alliance Theatre in Atlanta, was one of our candidates, and I was secretly rooting for her. Edith is something of a legend in the regional theater field, and I felt that her deep experience, national connections, and creativity in developing community programs would be great assets. But I confess that at the time, I would have been happy for my grandmother to be managing director if it meant I could share some of the workload.

Also in July, we had our second hearing before the Portland Development Commission. Norris and his staff had spent weeks putting together a proposal that would authorize the pursuit of the New Markets and Historic tax credits on our behalf. In this plan PDC would also chip in with a loan to help buy the building, but all of this was contingent upon our raising $2 million by September 30, less than three months away. After considerable discussion, gnashing of a few

> Great neighborhoods are places where people live, work and play in unique settings which are distinguished by their diversity, design and history. The redevelopment of the Armory into a world-class theater and community center is a leading example of why Portland's Pearl District is such a vibrant neighborhood.
>
> *Don Mazziotti,* Former Executive Director of the Portland Development Commission

Digging In *continued*

teeth, and the wringing of many hands, the proposal was approved by the commission. I'm not sure any of them expected us to raise the money.

Shortly thereafter, we met for the first time with the board of the Portland Family of Funds (PFF), the governing body created to oversee the Portland New Markets Fund and its pursuit and allocation of New Markets Tax Credits in Portland. The Armory would be the first project that PFF supported, so we had to convince them that we could make the project work. Hard questions, lots of interest, and a healthy amount of skepticism were all to be found at the table.

And with our eyes on September 30, fundraising moved into full swing. To put our challenge in perspective, the most PCS had ever raised in a year was $1.78 million. So to raise $2 million in ten weeks felt like a completely impossible task. But that's what we had to do.

The following weeks moved the design phase of the work from "what if" to "how?" Weekly meetings

Digging In *continued*

began with Gerding/Edlen (acting pro bono as project developer), and GBD who were still on as project architects. Landry & Bogan began to come in on a monthly basis to design and outfit the theaters.

Excavation became a topic of discussion. The original walls of the Armory only extended about four feet below the street (how it had stood all that time is a mystery). Significant structural support would have to be added for the building to hold everything we needed and to provide seismic upgrades. While Bob had initially balked at digging farther than necessary to shore up the foundation, Jack Bogan, the chief theater designer, felt strongly that locating the Studio Theater above the lobby was not going to work. He said it would make the lobby too squat, obscure the historic trusses, and make it impossible to isolate the space acoustically while leaving the historic roof in place. Jack's suggestion was that we consider excavating and put the Studio Theater underneath the mainstage theater. While excavation would be costly, it could also solve a number of other issues we were facing, including the acoustical challenges.

BLIND FAITH AND COMMON SENSE

Why the Armory, Why Now?

JULIE
VIGELAND

One never knows what the future holds. There are times when we push forward on blind faith. With others, it takes the courage of one's convictions. On the Armory project, I started with one and ended up with the other. Time and time again, as we worked to make the old Armory into the new home for Portland Center Stage, we were able to overcome problems - so often that we began to use the phrase *the stars aligned* when we spoke about the project. • I became involved with this project because as chair of the Center Stage board, I believed a new facility was the obvious next step for artistic and financial growth. Eventually, my motivation was fueled by the realization that this new theater was not only critical to the organization, but also to the Pearl neighborhood, to Portland, and to the theater community at large. Renovating the historic Armory building — a Portland landmark — into a theater with the highest of design and environmental standards, is a signature event for all of us. It will positively influence our cultural life, the vitality of our community, and the environment. We already know that it is stimulating other projects around the country. • People ask me what keeps me going. The truth is that whenever we ran up against a barrier, all I could think about was how far we had come. There were too many reasons to continue to move forward: Chris Coleman and I had led a strategic planning process for the theater that clearly outlined our space needs. The Keewaydin Report (from consultants who recommended a move to a new facility) had validated our beliefs and given a sense of urgency to our move. • The Armory had become available and we had it within our grasp. We were envisioning not just a home for Center Stage but a new community center and gathering place for Portland. Our goal of a platinum LEED building would bring visitors interested in green building solutions to Portland from far and near. We were changing the paradigm of theaters and were already being watched by theater companies across the nation. • I've spoken to hundreds of people about this project, and it resonates on so many levels with so many different groups. In the beginning, I was surprised by the incredible energy and support reflected back after telling our story. Theater people, philanthropists, business people, political leaders, and people I meet casually all want to hear more. Those from New York, Kansas City, Los Angeles, Seattle and other cities want to know how we've done it; they want to do the same thing. And when I share *those* stories with the Portland community, people here realize how important it is to support this project. This was a gift to our city that all should have the opportunity to be part of as funders, benefactors, and ultimately attendees. • We all win. Of course, I'm biased, but I think this dream project is just good, common sense.

Julie Vigeland is the former Chair of the Portland Center Stage Board and serves as the Chair and Manager of the Capital Campaign for the Gerding Theater at the Armory. She has lived in Portland for over 40 years and currently is a member of the Regional Arts and Culture Council Board, the Giving in Oregon Council, The Wessinger and Jackson Foundations, and the Multnomah Athletic Club Board.

INTIMATE AND COMFORTABLE

Sweating the Theater-Designing Details

ROSE STEELE,
JACK BOGAN,
HEATHER MCAVOY AND
JIM HULTQUIST

Landry & Bogan, Inc. became involved with Portland Center Stage (PCS) because the staff knew us through our work at the Oregon Shakespeare Festival — we were the consultants for the Angus Bowmer Theatre in the 1970s and the New Theatre completed in 2002. It was a good working relationship because we see ourselves as 'holding the pencil' for their concept of what their spaces needed to be — it's about their vision, not ours. PCS needed us to understand and articulate their needs and to represent them accurately to the architect while they continued to meet a demanding production schedule. • Professional companies know what they want, and Center Stage wanted less formality and a recessive space that would disappear when the house lights went down. As a theater group that does not focus on any one specific era or style, it needed a performance venue that didn't call attention to itself. In this context, the requirement is not for a great and original form-giver, but for an understanding that the production rather than the architecture is the star of the show. GBD Architects put together a team that understood this. • Simplicity, intimacy and comfort were priorities in the design along with an intent to emphasize the character of the old building and its new mission. • Our main objective was to house all the needed spaces within the existing building and the budget. Reusing the Armory building posed several challenges; most notably for us was how to create a stage tall enough for vertical movement of scenery below roof ties that couldn't be altered. The magnificent sloping roof of the Armory cuts away precious space, which demanded creative solutions from every designer involved in the project. In this case, L&B lowered the stage from the original concept design to maximize scenery capability. • Space constraints dictated the unusual design of the costume and prop construction area as well. These spaces are an afterthought in many theater plants, particularly older ones. They are frequently in "found spaces"— basements, old mechanical rooms, the former walk-in cooler of a WWII cafeteria building — and the PCS space wasn't much better. It's not much more than a wide spot in a hallway. This company makes most of its own costumes and props and needs ample, efficient and functional space. Production staff will spend hundreds of hours there for each production. The best solution was to create a two-level costume and prop studio with an elevator and stairs connecting them. • The completed facility will house administration, costume and prop construction and storage, rehearsal, and performance functions — all of PCS operations except scenery construction. The main theater space has 599 seats with 526 on the main floor and 71 in a small balcony. It includes an orchestra pit and overstage scenery capability. The studio theater is a flexible space seating 100 to 200 in various audience-performer relationships. All theatrical equipment systems are state of the art and custom designed for Center Stage's needs.

Landry & Bogan has been providing theater design consulting since 1971, and the current principals have been working together since 1987. They have worked for regional theater companies and educational and civic institutions on projects as large as 5000 seats and as small as 100 for the full range of performing arts.

FINANCING THE ARMORY

HERBERT F.
STEVENS

Old Building, New Resources

Herbert F. Stevens is a partner
with the national firm,
Nixon Peabody, LLP, and is
the leader of his firm's
New Markets Tax Credits and
Historic Tax Credit practice.

Because of the special circumstances of the Armory building and its desired use, the traditional options for financing were not feasible. The requirements of the project included a large capital outlay, preservation of a historic landmark, substantial costs for seismic work and a stipulation that the building be "green." In addition, the preferred use as a theater was not likely to generate as much revenue as a for-profit venture and would certainly not generate a steady stream of predictable revenue that could be financed by traditional lenders. • Acting as investment banker and financial developer, Norris Lozano and his team at Portland Family of Funds (PFF) brought a new federal tax credit to the project to attract private corporate equity: New Markets Tax Credits (NMTC), enacted in 2001 to stimulate business and commercial activity in low-income areas. The Armory project would be one of the first in the nation to use these new tax credits. • Goldman Sachs and Company had received an award of tax credits and was searching for deserving projects nationally. PFF helped the project obtain a sub-allocation from Todd Stern at Goldman Sachs and an equity investment from Zach Boyers at US Bancorp Community Development Corporation based in part on these credits. In addition to NMTCs, PFF layered in state Business Energy Tax Credits due to its green goals, and federal historic tax credits. The Armory was on the National Register of Historic Places and was located in what was then determined by the 2000 United States Census as a low-income neighborhood. Thus, it qualified for both types of federal tax credits. • The two federal tax credits each have strict requirements for the type of property or business that can be financed. The historic tax credit requires a building and a rehabilitation plan approved by state and federal historic officials. NMTC's require that the project serve a low-income area and offer significant community benefits such as the creation of jobs. Both tax credits also come with stringently enforced "recapture" provisions, which penalize investors who don't keep the properties in compliance for a seven- to nine-year period. • In order to receive the tax credits, investors, too, must comply with federal requirements. For this reason, PFF manages special compliance procedures required during construction and during operation. Only certain costs qualify, and every construction draw must be carefully structured. Loan repayments and project revenues also have to be monitored for program compliance. • In addition to gathering the investors and ensuring federal compliance, PFF also accomplished an important community service: It arranged to have financing paid down over time as the nonprofit sponsor, Portland Center Stage, raised money from charitable donors. Allowing PCS to develop a capital campaign over a longer period gives it time to engage and win support from the community.

CHET ORLOFF

Chet Orloff is director of the Pamplin Institute, an adjunct professor of Urban Studies and Planning at Portland State University, and Director-Emeritus of the Oregon Historical Society. He practices history with numerous public and private agencies and firms throughout the Northwest and serves on numerous local, state, and national committees and commissions relating to history, planning and urban design.

TENNIS, ANYONE?

Portland Stories

In 1962, I was at the Armory with some of the world's greatest tennis players when they came to Portland for a series of exhibition matches. · As a ball boy. · These were the men who had dominated the amateur sport and had pioneered the professional tour. Pancho Gonzales, Pancho Segura, Lewis Hoad and Jack Kramer, to name a few. I was asked, along with a group of other young players, to assist in two singles matches and a doubles event. A crowd of about 300 Portland tennis aficionados filled the same wooden benches used by spectators of professional wrestling events. It was cold in the Armory; a couple of the players continued to wear their sweaters throughout the evening. Before indoor tennis became common, a mid-winter tennis event like this one had special meaning for those of us locked into a summer sport. The touring pros had brought their own tarp tennis court. It was a singular evening for a 13 year old. ·

As ball retrievers, it was our job to chase down balls between points and toss them, with one bounce (we'd practiced the toss in a morning-long training match with two local champions), to our august guest players. Four of us stood behind the baseline while two crouched at the net (expecting at any moment to get hit by an errant serve or mispunched volley). During one long rally, while I was "playing" the net post, a ball hit the top of the net but made it over and the play continued. At the sound of the ball hitting the net, however, I reactively jumped into the fray and got caught in the middle of the court while the ball was still whizzing back and forth. The players seemed more amused than annoyed at the additional challenge of avoiding me while trying to win the point. · When the rally ended, I sprinted back to the end of the net and crouched as low as I could while the umpire admonished me and the other ball boys (and girls) to stay out of the field of play. A few members of the audience booed. Years after, my fellow competitors would bring up the time when "Orloff jumped the gun" and got involved in a rally — racketless — with the world's top tennis pros. Boxing matches; presidential appearances; carnivals; ball boys dodging 100-mile-an-hour serves from the wooden rackets of Kramer and Gonzales; Oregon soldiers preparing to sail off to the Philippines in the Spanish-American War; heavyweight wrestlers pounding each other into the mat; the workers at a local brewery stacking bottles of beer. What a dynamic and profoundly communitarian prologue for the stories now to be told within the carved Columbia River basalt walls of the Armory building by Portland Center Stage. The drama continues.

CH:4 THE GREEN PEARL:
Renovate Locally, Act Globally

IN THIS CHAPTER

A revelation occurs:
an arts manager links biodiversity
to audience development.
Consciousness-raising finds
a new vehicle in an old venue.

EPIPHANY

Meanwhile, I was struggling with the whole sustainability aspect of the project. Stuart Cowan, PDC's "green expert" had begun sitting in on our meetings, offering cheerful suggestions, and I was making his participation pretty difficult. But I was also slowly beginning to realize that I either had to find a way to get over myself and integrate the environmental stuff into the design, or I had to say it wasn't going to work. So in August, I scheduled a field trip with Stuart.

We met at the Ecotrust Building on NW Lovejoy and 10th Avenue. Ecotrust, or the Jean Vollum Natural Capital Center, is a very cool place. It was imagined as a building that would gather both for-profit and nonprofit ventures with missions related to creating a healthier environment, under one roof. The structure itself is also a beautiful example of sustainable design, and as the first LEED Gold rated building in Portland, it draws hundreds of thousands of visitors each year to the event center, retail shops and a farmers' market housed in the office building.

I loved the building the moment I walked in. The wide, irregular hardwood floors (created from the building's original walls), the attractive choice of materials in the conference room, the super-cool eco roof/gathering area up top, the video screens on the walls, the smell of Hot Lips Pizza wafting through the corridors — the whole building had a great feel. They had managed to make a center that physically expressed the philosophical mission of the place. And the juxtaposition

p112

Epiphany *continued*

of natural textures and recycled materials with very clean, contemporary finishes, felt very warm and very Portland-y to me. As you walked through the building you learned about many different aspects of environmental effort in the world, as well as other fun activities in the city.

This was a big "AHA!" moment for me. I suddenly saw that if Portland Center Stage's central goal was to reinvent its relationship with the community, and we were trying to do that in Portland, Oregon, the city that cares more about sustainability than any city on the planet, then *what better* way to make that happen than to become one of the leading examples of sustainable design in the Northwest? ANNNNNNND to become a place where Joe "I don't know anything about green stuff" Blow can interact with the sustainability story in a fun, informative, playful way. So, in essence, a building becomes a magnet for many, many different kinds of people. Our core mission will always be the theater-going experience, but I began to see that weaving the sustainable story into the building had the potential

Epiphany *continued*

to make the project significantly more resonant, more potent and more interesting. Not to mention redefine our relationship to the audience, to our space, and to the way people experience that space.

September 30 arrived; our $2 million had materialized from several major donors, and we sailed full steam ahead. The fall was crazy and fun with the success of *Batboy: The Musical* spreading the face of the lead actor Wade McCollum across every newspaper in town. Our press rep arranged for Wade to perform a number from the show in costume (including "bat" ears) before Portland City Council, and I will never forget the bizarre looks on the faces in chamber that day. Vera was totally into it; Commissioner Jim Francesconi shuffled through papers and didn't look up. But the folks in the audience waiting for their hearings were the best. They were completely mystified by the proceedings ("is this some politically incorrect championing of differently-abled people, or . . .") and didn't know whether it was appropriate to laugh or not. I was doubled over trying not to cackle too loudly.

We also had key meetings with Todd Stearn, a New Markets Tax Credits manager from Goldman Sachs, the investment banking firm in New York. At this point, Portland New Markets Fund had learned it had not received an allocation of tax credits, but Norris had learned that Goldman Sachs had been awarded $75 million in tax credits and was searching for an appropriate

> Goldman Sachs is proud to have partnered with Portland Center Stage, US Bank, and the Portland Family of Funds to support one of the city of Portland's premier cultural arts organizations. This project accomplishes everything the New Markets Tax Credits was meant to achieve: It makes economic sense for investors; it creates jobs and opportunity in a historically underserved community; and it spurs economic growth in an environmentally sustainable way.
>
> *Todd Stern.* Vice President of the Goldman Sachs Urban Investment Group

Epiphany *continued*

project. The requirements for this sub-allocation would be that the project cost more than $20 million, construction begin in the next six months, and a team be in place that could pull the project off. They were excited about the Armory, and it was beginning to sound like we might have a shot.

The common perception of New Markets Tax Credits at the time was that they were intended as funds for affordable housing projects. This was not correct, but as a new program it was easily misunderstood. What became clear in that first discussion with Goldman Sachs was that New Markets Tax Credits projects could be quite diverse if the full potential of the program were applied. We also learned that lots of great projects were languishing around the country.

(Since the Armory transaction closed, NMTCs have been used to help fund the restoration of the historic Meier & Frank Building into a hotel and new Macy's department store; to turn the boarded up Civic Apartment building into sustainable low-

Epiphany *continued*

income housing, condos, retail, green space and parking; to build a new medical office building for the Oregon Clinic in the Gateway neighborhood; to turn an empty lot on Martin Luther King, Jr. Boulevard into the Fremont Building and a vacant machine shop into Vanport Square Phase I in Northeast Portland; and to build a new drug rehabilitation facility for Union Gospel Mission in Old Town. Other Portland NMTC projects include a new elementary school, a new college building, even a new loan fund for small businesses in low-income areas. Ecotrust actually received a $50 million allocation to help fund sustainable logging practices in Oregon and Washington.)

During the same time frame we began meeting with Zach Boyers in US Bank's Community Development Corporation out of St. Louis. They seemed interested in making the construction loan, and purchasing the tax credits. But the question arose, "What if the project doesn't work? How would PCS make good on the loan?" We had no collateral to guarantee a loan. Portland Development Commission couldn't legally guarantee anything, so discussions began with the city to see if some kind of assurance could be arranged.

Now, this is a little arcane, but the line of discussion was critical. The city was not eager to wind up in a mess where taxpayers would end up paying for a project that didn't succeed. But there was a growing level of interest in helping make the Armory happen. And if positioned properly, the city's risk could be minimized. Once the building was complete, if the capital campaign was unfinished, we could leverage financing by using the $30 million theater as collateral. What the bank needed was some kind of formal agreement.

We spoke with Ken Rust, the city's chief financial officer, about asking for a "Moral Obligation," which would state that at the end

THE ARMORY IS AN OUTSTANDING EXPRESSION OF THE STRENGTH AND CREATIVITY OF PORTLAND'S GREEN BUILDING INDUSTRY. ECOTRUST AND THE ARMORY EXEMPLIFY HOW OLD HISTORIC BUILDINGS CAN BE ADAPTED TO MODERN FUNCTIONS WHILE RETAINING THEIR UNIQUE CHARACTER, DESPITE MANY BARRIERS, WHEN THE COMMUNITY DECIDES TO MAKE IT HAPPEN. FITTING THE NEW THEATER BUILDING INSIDE THE ARMORY CREATES AN ENTIRELY MODERN AND FUNCTIONAL SPACE WHILE PRESERVING THE STORY OF THE ARMORY AROUND IT. THAT REQUIRED CARE AND COMMITMENT, THE CAPABILITIES OF A PROJECT TEAM THAT HAD ALREADY SUCCESSFULLY COMPLETED OTHER LEED BUILDINGS IN THE BREWERY BLOCKS, AND THE LEADERSHIP OF GERDING/EDLEN'S DENNIS WILDE, WHO HAD RENOVATED THE REFRIGERATED WAREHOUSE THAT IS NOW THE SPLENDID WIEDEN + KENNEDY BUILDING.

Susan Anderson. Director of Portland's Office of Sustainable Developments

Epiphany *continued*

of 10 years, if PCS had not been able to pay off the remainder of the US Bank Loan, the city would help find options to finance the balance. There was no guarantee that the city would pay the balance, and there was no guarantee that the city would put a dollar into the project. That was enough for US Bank.

Halloween night 2003, *Batboy* opened to crazy, happy response — and Edith Love arrived as our new managing director. I was delighted by both events. A few weeks later we took our proposal before the city council for ratification, and with Vera giving it a hearty endorsement, the resolution to offer the "Moral Obligation" passed unanimously.

THE GREENING OF THE ARMORY

Hybrid Arts and the Culture of Sustainability

ARMORY VOICES:
Sustainability

STUART
COWAN

The Portland Armory is an experiment in growing a culture of sustainability. It is a community hub, a crossroads, a center for the arts, and an abandoned castle reinvented as an intelligent structure. I believe it will become a place of synthesis, where those who are busy reinventing cultural DNA will draw inspiration from the practical work of greening a city block by block. The stories from the stage will be refracted through another layer of story that seeps from walls and sidewalks, hinting at beneficial new relationships with water, energy, matter and community. • The Portland Armory represents a new kind of civic ecology, magnificent placemaking in the service of both community and nature. Portland Center Stage and dozens of other arts organizations will challenge our political, ethical, and aesthetic norms — all within the rich physical context of the Armory's own grand arc of historical and ecological restoration. Over time, hybrid arts may evolve here that reconnect us to the more-than-human world. These hybrid arts will generate their energy by cutting to the raw drama inherent in history, place, and everyday choices. The Portland Armory could become a place to explore the intersection of art and ecology, performance and community. •

As we approach an era of profound ecological constraints, every region has the opportunity to actively invest in a culture of sustainability that will allow it to become prosperous, equitable and resilient. Regions will flourish through a combination of social capital, sustainable commerce, and environmentally sensitive building and planning. The Armory will become an open-source node in Portland's regional sustainability operating system. By design, it will rapidly diffuse best practices at the building, neighborhood, and city scales to visitors from the region and beyond. The Portland Armory, by virtue of its exemplary green features, propelled by its interpretive displays and fueled by its innovative events programming, will help awaken our collective imagination of how to live well in this place. • Thanks to the generous vision of Portland Center Stage, the Armory will host a matrix of relationships between theater and the arts, urban design and sustainability, not a place for bland utopia or shrill ideology, but for the real drama of making a particular part of the world work. The Armory awaits, ready to mutate our world views, to inspire us and to give us a new Portland icon.

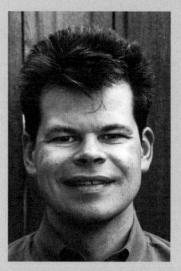

Stuart Cowan is a Managing Partner in Portland-based Autopoiesis, LLC, which delivers design, capacity and capital to sustainable businesses and green real estate projects internationally. He is the co-author of *Ecological Design*, received his doctorate in the new science of living systems from UC Berkeley, served as Research Director for Ecotrust, and was a Transaction Manager for Portland Family of Funds.

OLD, GREEN AND PLATINUM

Armory Wins Top Rating

ELAINE AYE

From the outset, it was clear that the restoration of the Armory could be an exemplary project to transform a historic building into a new national model in sustainable design. The sustainability goal for the project, LEED® Platinum, was virtually unheard of at the time of its submission for an award (there were only 12 Platinum projects in the world). Moreover, the Armory was slated to receive a 20% Historic Tax Credit from the federal government, the first LEED Platinum project to achieve this goal. • In order to satisfy the rigorous, and often competing criteria for Platinum certification on a building listed on the National Register of Historic Places, all the players brought a strong commitment to sustainable goals. Green Building Services helped foster synergies between the architectural, engineering and interior design disciplines to attain the necessary level of energy efficiency, indoor air quality, and water conservation required by a truly high-performance building. • To accomplish our goals, we often found ourselves at the leading edge of sustainable design, creating solutions that used the most contemporary technologies and materials available. For example, the Armory achieved optimal performance thanks to technical analyses generated by computational fluid dynamic (CFD) modeling, which allowed the team to verify performance assumptions. A few of the integrated measures in the Armory include:

• CFD modeling examined ways to provide effective ventilation and climate control in the building and evaluate new technologies, such as chilled beams for cooling. These chilled beams are supplied by a central water chilling plant that serves several buildings in the area.

• A displacement ventilation system was installed that provides conditioned air underneath the seats of the mainstage theater. This system distributes tempered fresh air efficiently at the human level, rather than flowing down from above, the method of the traditional A/C model.

• Rainwater falling on the building is captured in a 12,000-gallon cistern under the sidewalk. Once filtered, the water is used in toilets and urinals with low-flow fixtures. The building's comprehensive water-conservation strategies are expected to generate an 89% savings of potable water.

• Employee offices tucked into the "roof" area of the building are lit with skylights that enhance the atmosphere with natural daylight and improve energy efficiency. These and other energy savings will allow the Armory to operate at approximately a 30% energy savings from conventional new construction of the same scale. • With the project's inherent complexities of multiple public and private stakeholders, strict adherence to the historic preservation criteria and aggressive program requirements, the Armory's success demonstrates that with the right commitment and resources virtually any project can incorporate extensive sustainable measures.

Elaine Aye, IIDA, and Alan Scott, AIA, CSI; Principals, Green Building Services, come from the worlds of Interior Design and Architecture, respectively, and have helped lead Green Building Services to a national leadership position in the sustainable design industry.

ROUTING THE ELEMENTS

A High- and Low-Tech Production

BOB
SCHROEDER

Bob Schroeder is an Associate Principal with Glumac, a LEED Accredited Professional and a registered engineer with over 25 years experience.

The challenges encountered in the implementation of the modern Mechanical, Electrical, Plumbing and Technology systems (MEPT - the routing of air ducts, water pipes, conduits and cables within the structure) can best be understood by imagining both the widely varying uses of the spaces and the conflicting requirements of historic preservation and sustainable design. Offices, work areas, rehearsal spaces, stages, event lobbies and function spaces are spread across multiple floors, all requiring different types of cabling and equipment. Glumac's charge was to select equipment and fit MEPT systems together so that they performed optimally, worked in concert with other systems and design elements, and obeyed the historic and LEED requirements of the project.

The design of the sustainable air circulation and temperature control systems in the Armory's multiple spaces is a good example of this dynamic. The lobby has a radiant heating/cooling floor, along with displacement diffusers that deliver air at relatively warm temperatures and velocities (approximately 63° and 20 feet per minute). The main-stage theater seating utilizes under-floor ventilation for comfort and noise reduction. (Supporting the acoustical requirements of a theater meant using fan wall technology — multiple smaller fans in lieu of a large fan. Fan walls also eliminated the need for sound traps that would have been difficult to install, add pressure drop to the system, and increase motor load. Electronic filtration also reduced pressure drop.)   •   To achieve individual temperature control for the administrative offices, each individual workstation and adjacent support space has its own, user-adjustable floor diffuser. A smaller-than-normal underfloor space required an access system that combines ventilation air with distribution of electrical and telecom systems. Also, we selected an active, chilled beam, overhead cooling and heating system, with an auxiliary fan and integrated lighting to save energy and reduce visual bulk. Fortunately, chilled water was extended from the Brewery Blocks cooling plant, eliminating unsightly equipment on the roof. A sophisticated energy management system with a full measurement and verification plan allows for the fine-tuning of components over time.   •   To conserve water, a rainwater harvesting system channels rain through the drain system for storage in a 12,000 gallon underground cistern large enough to accommodate drought conditions in the summer. The water is filtered and sterilized before distribution to water closets, urinals and water sculpture in the new park. Low-flow fixtures are used throughout, and, in back-of-house private spaces, dual flush technology water closets are used.   •   Integrating telecommunications cabling and security systems provided unique challenges. Of particular interest is the video surveillance system: a single network cable transports video streams to a central networked server and powers the cameras. That reduced the overall use of raw materials, such as copper and polymers for cable, by 50 percent. This approach allows for access to the video system by the administration staff from any computer with access to their network, such as a home PC or even a handheld PDA.

AN ETHOS OF RENEWAL

A Theater Revisited and Refined

ARMORY VOICES:
Design

RANDY GRAGG

Maybe it all begins with the Bottle Bill. The famous 1971 law requiring a five-cent deposit on every soft drink and beer initiated a new relationship between Oregonians and their used containers. Suddenly "an empty" gained a second life: a refill, a reincarnation or, or at the very least, a nickel in your pocket.　•　It started with soda pops and beers and grew to architecture.　•　At least that's one way to understand the transformation of a 115-year-old brick armory building into The Gerding Theater at the Armory.　•　Indeed, look at the past 20 years of the city's major building projects, and you easily could get the idea that Portland is afraid of building anything new. As cities across the country commissioned new libraries, art museums, theaters and even the occasional city hall in bold new styles with marquee architects, Portland adopted an architectural strategy comparable to thrift-store shopping and resoling old shoes. Call it the Bottle Bill Era of Portland architecture.　•　To be sure, many of our old buildings, sturdy and refillable as the chunky Coca Cola bottles of old, proved well suited to the cause. Consider, for instance, the 1914 Multnomah County Library. Conceived in 1913 by librarian Mary Frances Isom and architect A.E. Doyle as one of the first open-plan libraries in the country — a proto-Modern "machine for books" — it proved beautifully retrofitable in 1997 as the social-and-technological hub libraries need to be now. So too, the 1895 Portland City Hall, which proved gracefully suited to the needs of a new century — once the architects tore out most of the previous century's remodeling.　•　Yet, the Armory's redo goes beyond any obvious urge to preserve such classic civic landmarks. It joins a series of Portland buildings — many of them fairly mundane by the standards of their day — that the Bottle Bill ethic has turned into landmarks. For instance, when the environmental organization Ecotrust decided to build its first headquarters, it could have created a demonstration project for the most advanced green technologies.

Instead it turned a rundown 1895 railroad warehouse into a homey clubhouse for the city burgeoning ecological movement. Even more dramatically, the globally renowned ad agency, Wieden + Kennedy, working with a then largely unproven architectural firm, Allied Works, created the city's most internationally celebrated work of architecture in half a century — inside a decrepit 1910 paint warehouse that for years had been standing, as engineers like to say, "out of habit."　•　Those are big, expensive projects in which humdrum vernacular buildings have been imbued with potent new civic and creative pride. But Portland's redo culture also reaches well below the monumental. Consider the work of the brothers McMenamin who have converted everything from old theaters to an elementary school and a state mental hospital into ecstatically popular brewpubs. Consider the Rebuilding Center with more than 20,000 square feet of salvaged building parts housed in a shed made out of reused windows — a veritable cathedral to the

Randy Gragg is the Architecture and Urban Design writer for *The Oregonian*. A longer version of this essay was published in *The Oregonian*, September 24, 2006.

we-redo ethic. • With the Armory-cum-Center-Stage project, however, Portland may be outdoing its own traditions. As a historic edifice, its jaunty, castle-like appearance looks almost Disney-like to us today, but it sprouted from a weird merging of fear and fashion. In the 1880s, Portland joined cities across the country that built armories for local militias formed to quell insurrections — mostly riots over everything from bread shortages to the draft to labor conditions. In Portland's case, early 1880s riots against the Chinese rallied citizens to the cause of an armory. As Robert M. Fogelson, a historian of armories, has noted, fear of class warfare was so pervasive in America's urban areas, the paranoia coined a popular phrase, "the volcano under the city." • Ironically, no shot was ever fired from the First Regiment Armory's gun slots. The city's volunteer army, in effect, played "fort," doing marching drills, dining and hobnobbing. In the wilds of an open Western city like Portland, the Armory became a kind of informal finishing school for young men, in the words of its chief promoter, Judge George H. Williams, to "acquire the habit of correct deportment." But as Portland's upper class cultivated new training grounds at the Arlington Club and Masonic Temple, the Armory gradually shifted to being an events center, primarily for circuses, big-time wrestling and boxing. In 1968, as a beer-keg warehouse, the building went into hiding beneath boarded windows and white paint. • But now the old Armory has been resurrected from its slumber, filled with state-of-the-art performing arts facilities and engineered to be the greenest cultural facility and historic rehab yet done in the country. On one level it has essentially become a classier and more overt version of what it really was for most of its life: a theater. On another, it is simply the most ambitious example yet of the Bottle Bill tradition of the refill.

A MODEL PROJECT

Community Benefits, New Partnerships

ARMORY VOICES:
Development

ZACHARY BOYERS

US Bancorp Community Development Corporation (USBCDC), a subsidiary of US Bank with investments of $3.0 billion, is based in St. Louis. It is a leading investor in Affordable Housing, Historic and New Markets Tax Credits throughout the country. • Though many people involved in the Portland Armory project had spent countless hours over many months overcoming numerous obstacles through the deal structuring and underwriting process, it was not until a January visit to Portland that I recognized the importance of the project to the city and the sincere commitment of the partners involved. It was then that I decided that USBCDC should make every effort to be a part of this magnificent redevelopment. • Our firm's multifaceted investment in the Portland Armory transaction was strategically sound for a variety of reasons. Not only did the opportunity fit within our investment risk parameters, but it also strongly addressed our core values: to make investments designed to provide substantial and sustainable community benefits. We supported this project because it promised to preserve and revitalize a historic structure, support the arts, and create jobs and economic development through substantial support of minority- and women-owned businesses. • Furthermore, environmentally conscientious construction and design elements make this a signature project for progressive thinking of the finest sort, and we are pleased to be a part of it. Lastly, the Armory transaction closed when the NMTC program was in its true infancy. In this way, it challenged sharp minds to think more sharply than ever so that the Armory would be a standard-setter for the power of the NMTC and the realization of its mission. The quality of the commitment made by many on this Portland Armory project is unique and bodes well for the Armory's impact on the community and for future projects like it.

Zachary Boyers is
Director of Historic Investments,
Senior Vice President,
US Bancorp Community
Development Corporation

A LASTING LEGACY

What Platinum Looks Like

Many factors contributed to the LEED Platinum rating of the Gerding Theater at the Armory. The features highlighted here are representative of dozens that contribute to improved indoor air quality, temperature and user comfort; high level of recycling; reduced impact on landfill, sewer systems and use of fossil fuels; maximum use of natural light; ongoing testing and optimization; and sustainable building maintenance processes that make the building a healthy place to work and visit.

This drawing was created through collaboration by GBD Architects, Green Building Services, Hoffman Construction, Glumac Engineering, Murase Associates and Portland Family of Funds.

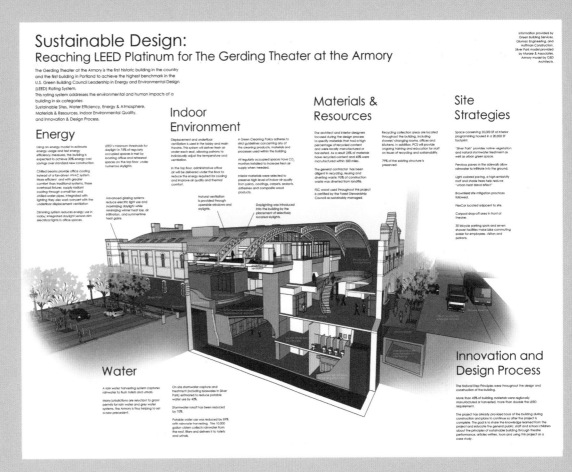

Sustainable Design:
Reaching LEED Platinum for The Gerding Theater at the Armory

The Gerding Theater at the Armory is the first historic building in the country and the first building in Portland to achieve the highest benchmark in the U.S. Green Building Council Leadership in Energy and Environmental Design (LEED) Rating System.

This rating system addresses the environmental and human impacts of a building in six categories: Sustainable Sites, Water Efficiency, Energy & Atmosphere, Materials & Resources, Indoor Environmental Quality, and Innovation & Design Process.

Information provided by Green Building Services, Glumac Engineering, and Hoffman Construction. Silver Park model provided by Murase & Associates. Armory model by GBD Architects.

Energy

Using an energy model to estimate energy usage and test energy efficiency measures, the building is expected to achieve 30% energy cost savings over standard new construction.

Chilled beams provide office cooling instead of a fan-driven HVAC system. More efficient and with greater comfort than traditional systems, these overhead fans supply radiant cooling through a small fan and chilled water pipes. Integrated with lighting they also work concert with the underfloor displacement ventilation.

Dimming system reduces energy use in lobby. Integrated daylight sensors dim electrical lights in office spaces.

LEED's minimum threshold for daylight in 75% of regularly occupied spaces is met by locating office and rehearsal spaces on the top floor under numerous skylights.

Advanced glazing systems reduce electric light use and maximizing daylight while minimizing winter heat loss, air infiltration, and summertime heat gains.

Indoor Environment

Displacement and underfloor ventilation is used in the lobby and main theatre. This system will deliver fresh air under each seat, allowing patrons to individually adjust the temperature and ventilation.

In the top floor, administrative office air will be delivered under the floor to reduce the energy required for cooling and improve air quality and thermal comfort.

Natural ventilation is provided through operable windows and skylights.

A Green Cleaning Policy adheres to strict guidelines concerning any of the cleaning products, materials and processes used within the building.

All regularly occupied spaces have CO_2 monitors installed to increase fresh air supply when needed.

Daylighting was introduced into the building by the placement of selectively located skylights.

Materials & Resources

The architect and interior designers focused during the design process to specify materials that had a high percentage of recycled content and were locally manufactured or harvested. As a result 25% of materials have recycled content and 65% were manufactured within 500 miles.

Interior materials were selected to preserve high level of indoor air quality from paints, coatings, carpets, sealants, adhesives and composite wood products.

The general contractor has been diligent in recycling, reusing and diverting waste: 95% of construction waste was diverted from landfills.

FSC wood used throughout this project is certified by the Forest Stewardship Council as sustainably managed.

Site Strategies

Space conserving 55,000 SF of interior programming housed in a 20,000 SF footprint.

"Silver Park" provides native vegetation and natural stormwater treatment as well as urban green space.

Pervious pavers in the sidewalk allow rainwater to infiltrate into the ground.

Light colored paving, a high-emissivity roof and shade trees help reduce "urban heat island effect."

Brownfield site mitigation practices followed.

FlexCar located adjacent to site.

Carpool drop-off area in front of theater.

30 bicycle parking spots and seven shower facilities make bike commuting easier for employees, visitors and patrons.

Water

A rain water harvesting system captures rainwater to flush toilets and urinals.

Many jurisdictions are reluctant to grant permits for rain water and grey water systems. The Armory is thus helping to set a new precedent.

On site stormwater capture and treatment (including bioswales in Silver Park) estimated to reduce potable water use by 65%.

Stormwater runoff has been reduced by 70%.

Potable water use was reduced by 69% with rainwater harvesting. The 10,000 gallon cistern collects rainwater from the roof, filters and delivers it to toilets and urinals.

Innovation and Design Process

The Natural Step Principles were throughout the design and construction of the building.

More than 65% of building materials were regionally manufactured or harvested, more than double the LEED requirement.

The project has already provided tours of the building during construction and plans to continue so after the project is complete. The goal is to share the knowledge learned from the project and educate the general public, staff and school children about the principles of sustainable building through theatre performance, articles written, tours and using this project as a case study.

PASSING THE TEST
Top Grade in a Tough Class

Green Building Services	Armory - Portland Center Stage	LEED® Scorecard of 9/29/2006

53		**14**	**Total Project Score**		Possible Points	**69**

Certified 26 to 32 points   Silver 33 to 38 points   Gold 39 to 51 points   Platinum 52 or more points

Sustainable Sites — Possible Points 14 — (11 / 3)

Y	?	N			
Y			Prereq 1	Erosion & Sedimentation Control	
1			Credit 1	Site Selection	1
1			Credit 2	Urban Redevelopment	1
1			Credit 3	Brownfield Redevelopment	1
1			Credit 4.1	Alternative Transportation, Public Transportation Access	1
1			Credit 4.2	Alternative Transportation, Bicycle Storage & Changing Rooms	1
1			Credit 4.3	Alternative Transportation, Alternative Fuel Refueling Stations	1
1			Credit 4.4	Alternative Transportation, Parking Capacity	1
		1	Credit 5.1	Reduced Site Disturbance, Protect or Restore Open Space	1
		1	Credit 5.2	Reduced Site Disturbance, Development Footprint	1
1			Credit 6.1	Stormwater Management, Rate and Quantity	1
1			Credit 6.2	Stormwater Management, Treatment	1
1			Credit 7.1	Landscape & Exterior Design to Reduce Heat Islands Non-Roof	1
1			Credit 7.2	Landscape & Exterior Design to Reduce Heat Islands Roof	1
		1	Credit 8	Light Pollution Reduction	1

Water Efficiency — Possible Points 5 — (5)

Y	?	N			
1			Credit 1.1	Water Efficient Landscaping, Reduce by 50%	1
1			Credit 1.2	Water Efficient Landscaping, No Potable Use or No Irrigation	1
1			Credit 2	Innovative Wastewater Technologies	1
1			Credit 3.1	Water Use Reduction, 20% Reduction	1
1			Credit 3.2	Water Use Reduction, 30% Reduction	1

Energy & Atmosphere — Possible Points 17 — (10 / 5)

Y	?	N			
Y			Prereq 1	Fundamental Building Systems Commissioning	
Y			Prereq 2	Minimum Energy Performance	
Y			Prereq 3	CFC Reduction in HVAC&R Equipment	
2			Credit 1.1	Optimize Energy Performance, 20% New / 10% Existing	2
2			Credit 1.2	Optimize Energy Performance, 30% New / 20% Existing	2
2			Credit 1.3	Optimize Energy Performance, 40% New / 30% Existing	2
		1	Credit 1.4	Optimize Energy Performance, 50% New / 40% Existing	2
		1	Credit 1.5	Optimize Energy Performance, 60% New / 50% Existing	2
		1	Credit 2.1	Renewable Energy, 5%	1
		1	Credit 2.2	Renewable Energy, 10%	1
		1	Credit 2.3	Renewable Energy, 20%	1
1			Credit 3	Additional Commissioning	1
1			Credit 4	Ozone Depletion	1
1			Credit 5	Measurement & Verification	1
1			Credit 6	Green Power	1

Materials & Resources — Possible Points 13 — (8 / 5)

Y	?	N			
Y			Prereq 1	Storage & Collection of Recyclables	
1			Credit 1.1	Building Reuse, Maintain 75% of Existing Shell	1
		1	Credit 1.2	Building Reuse, Maintain 100% of Existing Shell	1
		1	Credit 1.3	Building Reuse, Maintain 100% Shell & 50% Non-Shell	1
1			Credit 2.1	Construction Waste Management, Divert 50%	1
1			Credit 2.2	Construction Waste Management, Divert 75%	1
		1	Credit 3.1	Resource Reuse, Specify 5%	1
		1	Credit 3.2	Resource Reuse, Specify 10%	1
1			Credit 4.1	Recycled Content, Specify 5%	1
1			Credit 4.2	Recycled Content, Specify 10%	1
1			Credit 5.1	Local/Regional Materials, 20% Manufactured Locally	1
1			Credit 5.2	Local/Regional Materials, of 20% Above, 50% Harvested Locally	1
		1	Credit 6	Rapidly Renewable Materials	1
1			Credit 7	Certified Wood	1

Indoor Environmental Quality — Possible Points 15 — (14 / 1)

Y	?	N			
Y			Prereq 1	Minimum IAQ Performance	
Y			Prereq 2	Environmental Tobacco Smoke (ETS) Control	
1			Credit 1	Carbon Dioxide (CO_2) Monitoring	1
1			Credit 2	Increase Ventilation Effectiveness	1
1			Credit 3.1	Construction IAQ Management Plan During Construction	1
1			Credit 3.2	Construction IAQ Management Plan Before Occupancy	1
1			Credit 4.1	Low-Emitting Materials, Adhesives & Sealants	1
1			Credit 4.2	Low-Emitting Materials, Paints	1
1			Credit 4.3	Low-Emitting Materials, Carpet	1
1			Credit 4.4	Low-Emitting Materials, Composite Wood	1
1			Credit 5	Indoor Chemical & Pollutant Source Control	1
1			Credit 6.1	Controllability of Systems, Perimeter	1
1			Credit 6.2	Controllability of Systems, Non-Perimeter	1
1			Credit 7.1	Thermal Comfort, Comply with ASHRAE 55-1992	1
1			Credit 7.2	Thermal Comfort, Permanent Monitoring System	1
1			Credit 8.1	Daylight & Views, Daylight 75% of Spaces	1
		1	Credit 8.2	Daylight & Views, Views for 90% of Spaces	1

Innovation & Design Process — Possible Points 5 — (5)

Y	?	N			
1			Credit 1.1	Innovation in Design: Educational Outreach	1
1			Credit 1.2	Innovation in Design: Green Housekeeping	1
1			Credit 1.3	Exemplary Performance: WEc3	1
1			Credit 1.4	Exemplary Performance: MRc5.1	1
1			Credit 2	LEED™ Accredited Professional	1

U S Green Building Council	Scorecard	LEED® Calculator 2.1

The Leadership in Energy and Environmental Design (LEED) Green Building Rating System™, sponsored by the US Green Building Council (USGBC) is the nationally accepted benchmark for the design, construction, and operation of high-performance green buildings. The program recognizes performance in five key areas of human and environmental health: sustainable site development, water savings, energy efficiency, materials selection, and indoor environmental quality. The LEED Scorecard (The Armorys is shown here) is the document the USGBC uses as a first gate to determine the green building achievements that a project team believes it has attained. A confirmed score of 52 LEED points denotes a Platinum rating; The Gerding Theater at the Armory received 53 points, the first time a building on the National Register of Historic Places has achieved this performance level.

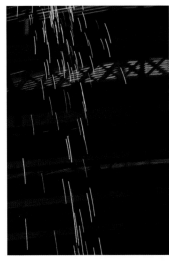

CH:5 INTELLIGENT DESIGN:
Authenticity, Integrity, Risk

IN THIS CHAPTER

Chris Coleman stages PCS's most controversial play, launches a multi-million dollar capital campaign, and challenges the division between performer and audience. All this while the Armory debate becomes very public.

THE CONTROVERSY 2004 broke with storms on several fronts. We were in rehearsal for *The Merchant of Venice*, a production by Hungarian director Robi Alfoldi. In January of 2000, I had been invited by the Center for International Theatre Development to travel to Budapest to see theater and meet young directors who could work in English. Traveling to a former Soviet-bloc country like Hungary was absolutely fascinating at this point in history. With the political changes still so very new, the entire economic, social and cultural systems were being reinvented and there was no telling where they were going to land.

But watching plays in Hungarian six time zones away from home can present challenges. You're running all day long, it's cold outside, you finally sit down in a dark, cozy theater and actors start talking in a foreign language. Heads nod. Snoring is heard. But the fourth night I was there (with a small group of American artistic leaders) we saw a production of *The Merchant of Venice* in this 200-seat theater that had been arranged with the action in the middle of the room and the audience stretched down either side. It was riveting.

Completely contemporary in tone and dress, the play began with a group of wild young people intensely dancing in a bar. Chock-full of homemade music videos, and highlighting the love triangle between Antonio, Bassanio and Portia — the production turned the play on its head. Robi Alfoldi, the dynamic young director, had chosen the piece in an effort to speak to the intolerance for "the

The Controversy *continued*

other" that had emerged in Hungarian society since the political changes. Under Communist rule, *Merchant* had been banned as too inflammatory, so Robi's production was the first in 40 years. It had been a sensation, and we could see why.

One of Robi's central choices was to make the relationship between Antonio and Bassanio romantic (they profess their affection for each other throughout Shakespeare's text, so it's not such a stretch). In Hungary, their scenes together were quite sexy (as were all the relationships actually), but not so much sexier than our production of *Flesh and Blood*.

We spent two years locating funding for the production, arranging a design team, and working on Robi's visa (which was nearly impossible to acquire, given new restrictions from Homeland Security). Back in Portland, I walked into the technical rehearsal (where you add lights and sound), and saw that Antonio and Bassanio's first scene, which had been played in underwear in Hungary, was now completely in the buff. The scene was potent enough in its European version,

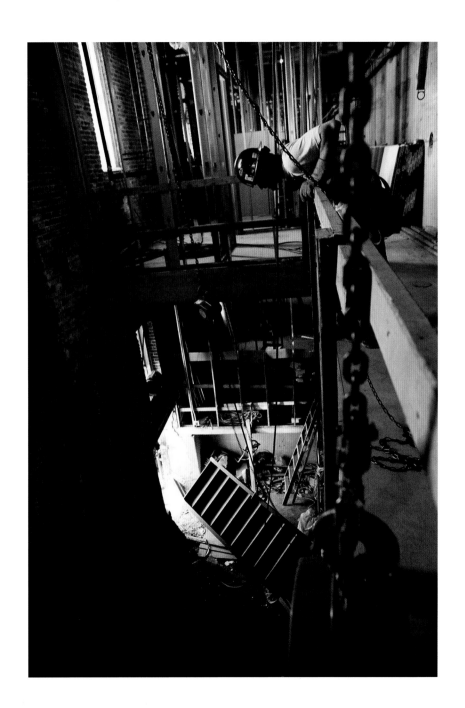

The Controversy *continued*

but now that these two amorous guys were naked and right downstage in the lovely Newmark Theatre — it was a different experience altogether. I felt that the nudity was handled pretty tastefully, but many of our audience members had a different assessment.

That same weekend a blizzard blasted the city, stranding people in their homes, shutting down buses and trains. Most of our staff called to say they couldn't get in. Having spent two years in grad school in Pittsburgh, I pulled on my Batboy boots (courtesy of Dr. Martens) and trudged through the snow to the theater.

On the same day, *Willamette Week* featured a huge picture of the Armory with the cover story entitled: "The Great White Hoax." My stomach turned over about five times. I knew that the paper's leading reporter had been working on a story as he had spoken with most of the project's leadership. But I was shocked by the blatant inaccuracies the article contained, and by the fact that the story warranted the cover. I mean, we were trying to build a theater. In most cities I'd lived in, to make the cover of the alternative weekly the sheriff had to murder his wife or something.

We joked that perhaps no one would read it because of the snowstorm. Little did we know how many people actually take the time to read *Willamette Week*. There were three primary points of misinformation in the article: 1) the implication that the Armory was equivalent to PGE Park, a previous public-private partnership that had left the city holding the bag for construction costs, and that if we went belly up, the city would end up paying for the project (never the case); 2) that the New Markets Tax Credits should have been invested in a needier part of the city (Not an invalid point, theoretically. But, as I stated earlier, Portland New Markets Fund had tried unsuccessfully to attract those dollars for projects in other areas. More importantly, the sub-allocation that we would receive would NOT have gone to

another project in Portland because of the very particular restrictions at Goldman Sachs, the main one being that at that moment there was not another project in the city that was large enough or close to being ready to compete for the allocation); and 3) that the transaction was a sweetheart deal lining Bob Gerding's pocket. Not only had Bob wanted to keep his personal donations — which were and still are the largest individual contributions we received — anonymous; his company had also agreed to donate $750,000 in project developer fees to the deal. The reality was that Bob's pocketbook was keeping the project afloat. To say that we were floored, angry and bewildered would put it quite mildly. Then *Merchant* opened.

Merchant of Venice was the most controversial production I've been a part of in 18 years of running theaters. We had done shows with nudity before. We had done shows with adult content before. We had even done shows with gay characters before. But this was new. Perhaps it was the fact that the production's sexual content was in a Shakespeare play that set people off. We thought we had warned people 100 times over

p138

about what to expect, but many people complained they weren't warned. Or, that when we said there would be nudity, that it would be female nudity. Not lying. Some people loved the extensive use of video in the show, others despised it. Everybody in the city was talking about it, for good or for bad. We, of course, sold a ton of single tickets and had a fantastic run. But we also lost at least 500 subscribers as a result of the production, we lost a few major donors, and at least one major foundation chose not to participate in the Capital Campaign because of the show.

Now, I've never been particularly afraid of controversy. I think that if you are going to talk about the things a society really cares about, you always risk being controversial. But, had I known that *Merchant* was going to light the fire it did, would I have chosen to produce it in the middle of a capital campaign? Who knows? Hindsight is 20/20.

> Now, I've never been particularly afraid of controversy. I think that if you are going to talk about the things a society really cares about, you always risk being controversial. But, had I known that *Merchant* was going to light the fire it did, would I have chosen to produce it in the middle of a capital campaign? Who knows? Hindsight is 20/20.
>
> *Chris Coleman*

What the controversy highlighted for me was the growing tension between "progressive Portland" and "conservative Portland." The city, founded by New England bankers, is one of the oldest on the West Coast and has traditionally been risk averse. The economy was long driven by natural resource-based industries. With the rise of high tech in the 1980s, the growth of the creative economy, and consistently progressive political leadership during the past 30 years, the face of the city has become more liberal. But the

OUR FIRM'S MULTIFACETED INVESTMENT IN THE PORTLAND ARMORY TRANSACTION WAS STRATEGICALLY SOUND FOR A VARIETY OF REASONS. NOT ONLY DID THE OPPORTUNITY FIT WITHIN OUR INVESTMENT RISK PARAMETERS, BUT IT ALSO STRONGLY ADDRESSED OUR CORE VALUES: TO MAKE INVESTMENTS DESIGNED TO PROVIDE SUBSTANTIAL AND SUSTAINABLE COMMUNITY BENEFITS. WE SUPPORTED THIS PROJECT BECAUSE IT PROMISED TO PRESERVE AND REVITALIZE A HISTORIC STRUCTURE, SUPPORT THE ARTS, AND CREATE JOBS AND ECONOMIC DEVELOPMENT THROUGH SUBSTANTIAL SUPPORT OF MINORITY- AND WOMEN-OWNED BUSINESSES. FURTHERMORE, ENVIRONMENTALLY CONSCIENTIOUS CONSTRUCTION AND DESIGN ELEMENTS MAKE THIS A SIGNATURE PROJECT FOR PROGRESSIVE THINKING OF THE FINEST SORT, AND WE ARE PLEASED TO BE A PART OF IT. THE QUALITY OF THE COMMITMENT MADE BY MANY ON THIS PORTLAND ARMORY PROJECT IS UNIQUE AND BODES WELL FOR THE ARMORY'S IMPACT ON THE COMMUNITY AND FOR FUTURE PROJECTS LIKE IT.

Zachary Boyers. Director of Historic Investments, Senior Vice President, US Bancorp Community Development Corporation

tension between those two images of Portland remains taut and real.

The press started to turn around that spring. An editorial from *The Oregonian* supported the carefully thought out public/private relationship devised for the Armory. They seemed to understand that the city had tried to learn from the lessons of PGE Park. Architecture critic Randy Gragg wrote a well-researched spread in Sunday's *Oregonian* about the project's aspirations, rebutting most of the misinformation in the *Willamette Week* article. It didn't dispel the myths that first *Willamette Week* article created, but it began to level the playing field a bit. Somehow the project managed to move forward; while all this was playing out in the papers, blogs and cocktail parties across town, Portland Family of Funds closed the deal in April, 2004.

Despite the controversies, large and small, our overall attendance for the season was up 18%. Perhaps most encouraging: we had attracted 1,200 subscribers under the age of 30; and a full 36% of our single-ticket buyers were now between the ages of 24 and 40.

THE USER EXPERIENCE

Norris knew that the leadership at PCS was focused on designing the theater spaces, and he began to encourage more proactive work to assure that the whole building would resonate for the community. After a West Coast Request For Proposal, he hired the local design team The Felt Hat over a dozen firms with clients that included companies like Nike, Disney, and FedEx. Felt Hat's particular expertise was unearthing creative ideas for community engagement. In April PCS leadership and PFF leadership gathered to hear Felt Hat's ideas about how to jazz up the public spaces in the Armory. We all had a sense that we wanted the theater-going experience to be more fun than it had traditionally been. But were there other design choices we could make or activities we could organize that would welcome the community in on a daily basis?

The chief players at The Felt Hat were Don Rood (who studied graphic design at Cooper Union) and Thom Walters (an organizational psychologist and cultural anthropologist who had spent many years p144

PORTLANDERS WANT THINGS THAT ARE CHARAC-
TERISTIC OF THE CITY AND ITS OWN DISTINCT CULTURE.
THEY DO NOT WANT THINGS THAT ARE SLAVISHLY
COPIED FROM OTHER PLACES. IN OTHER WORDS, THEY
WANT NO BORROWED VALUES. IF SOMETHING MAKES
SENSE AND HAS MEANING, THEN PORTLANDERS WILL
INVITE IT HERE. THEY ARE SUSPICIOUS OF GROWTH
FOR ITS OWN SAKE BECAUSE THEY WANT THINGS
THAT WILL STAND THE TEST OF TIME. PORTLANDERS
ARE MORE INTERESTED IN QUALITY THAN QUANTITY.

The Felt Hat, in their final report "Designing
and Experience: The Portland Armory"

The User Experience *continued*

at Wieden + Kennedy), and they conducted research about why Portlanders gather, what their perceptions of the Armory Project were, and what people might want out of an experience in the building. Thankfully, the messages that came back resonated strongly with what we were hoping to achieve. Portlanders wanted something authentic, something they could interact with at their leisure. They wanted opportunities to socialize, to learn about the building, and to find out what else was happening in Portland. They wanted an adventure, a sense of surprise. And they wanted it to be authentically Portland.

Felt Hat's initial recommendations about how to create a dynamic user experience included ideas both grand (a huge candelabra that would be lit every night at sunset), and intimate (glass bricks that "revealed" the history embedded in the walls of the building). They integrated existing concepts for the space (interactive media and Vera Katz Park along the building's north side) and brought forth a great many new ones that deeply affected all our thinking. And while we had no clue how to pay for any of them, the ideas were thrilling. Thinking "outside the box" in terms of creating an interactive experience for our guests was both exciting and daunting.

> The Portland Armory inspires the anticipation of discovery. The Armory is a place where stories will be told, with a standing invitation for anyone to get to know them. The stories are about Portland theater, history, sustainability and community. The experience of the Armory is the anticipation of discovering the next story.
>
> *The Felt Hat*

After all, this is not necessarily the realm of expertise for arts organizations. We're great at putting on performances, selling concessions, reserving tickets. But how to create a level of energy in the public spaces that lives and breathes beyond the hours of performance was something no theater I had encountered had yet sustained.

The User Experience *continued*

Dan Wieden (of Wieden + Kennedy) had been invited as an innocent bystander to respond to the presentation, and he suggested that all our efforts be channeled through the voice of the theater. He reflected that we are fundamentally an art form that tells stories, and whether we wanted to tell the story of what is happening next at the theater, the story of the history of the building, the story of how we built this cool sustainable project, or what is going on culturally in the city, we had to do that through the original, idiosyncratic voice of Portland Center Stage — an irreverent, often funny, usually casual and thought-provoking voice.

Meanwhile, our fundraising continued. Julie and I coaxed donors through the Armory when the floor was still concrete and said, "Soon there will be a big hole in the ground," and when there was a big hole in the ground, we'd say "Soon there will be walls on the side." And when there were walls on the side, we'd say, "Pretty soon you'll be able to see the floors being poured," and when the floors had been poured we would say, "Next month the scaf- p148

The User Experience *continued*

folding comes down and they'll start painting."

Watching the construction process day by day was a revelation. Our project manager at Hoffman Construction said it was the most complex project they had ever worked on, and the coordination of the electricians, painters, welders, carpenters, acousticians, masons, etc., was symphonic in its precision. You came in one day, and all the concrete for an entire floor had been poured. You came back two days later, and an elevator shaft had appeared. Two days later, skylights appeared in the roof. It gave me deep, deep respect for the builders in our community.

I was particularly moved when we were able to give Vera Katz a tour of the building. After twelve years as the city's mayor, the entire community had watched Vera struggle with breast cancer during her final year in office. She had fought through, and survived longer than any of her doctors anticipated, but she was definitely a little slower than in the old days. She arrived at the Armory smiling, wobbled slowly but cheerfully up the steps and ordered me to fix her hardhat so that

WE BROUGHT THE BEAMS UP THE STREET ON AN ANGLE, TUCKED
THEM THROUGH THE APERTURE WITH LITERALLY AN INCH TO SPARE,
AND PUT THEM ON A FLATCAR TROLLEY WITH A 40' TRACK WE'D BUILT
TO TRANSITION THE BEAMS INSIDE. THEN THE CRANE PUT THEM IN
PLACE FOR THE WELDERS, WHO MADE SHOWERS OF SPARKS THAT
WERE 60 FEET LONG. IT WAS A THRILLING DAY.
Pat Conrad. Project Superintendent, Hoffman Construction

it fit her head more comfortably. She "ooohed" and "ahhhhed" and asked hard, cranky questions.

And on the way out, the two construction workers who had been kind enough to operate the freight elevator for us said, "Take care of yourself, Vera." She thanked them, and joked, "You know, without me, you wouldn't have this job!" We all laughed.

Having Edith on board as managing director made a huge difference for the operations of the theater. But it also brought a level of attention and detail to our plans for the building and for expanding education and outreach opportunities.

Edith's eye was always looking out for the patron. She wanted to make certain that we were making it easy for people to use the building in practical ways, and that we were designing in a way that would help the building pay for itself once it opened. She fought doggedly, vociferously and unyieldingly for more women's restrooms than men's (there are twice as many, if you are curious); made certain the coat-check area would work with the box office; and asked for a "dog watering" station in the Vera Katz Park. She and Rose Riordan (our associate artistic director) jointly arrived at the notion of surrounding the rehearsal hall with our administrative offices, and putting a kitchen in the middle. It is a simple, and obvious solution — but one that happens rarely in the American theater.

In January of 2005, we had an on-site visit with Diane Ragsdale, program officer from the Mellon Foundation. Diane became so excited about the experiments we were considering in the lobbies, that she said, "If you pull this off, it could become a new model for how arts organizations interface with their communities around the country." That hadn't necessarily been our plan, but it was an affirmation of our core ideas. Then in October of 2005, the design team invited Ed Schlossberg from New York to brainstorm

The User Experience *continued*

with us on how to make certain the public spaces did what we wanted them to do. Why another consultant? By this time we had spent months thinking up different activities, or interactive media we could program to activate the lobby. But Bob Gerding stopped and said, "You know what, nobody has ever succeeded at this before, and I know that museums have thrown a lot of money at it. So before we finalize our plans, we need to test them against somebody who knows more about this than we do."

Ed began his career designing the "experience" aspect of children's museums, and has now become one of the world's experts in helping make interactive experiences happen. Among his claims to fame is helping orchestrate the redesign of Times Square. Ed came in for two days in October of 2005, and after listening to all of our ideas, intentions and dreams, he cut to the chase. He said, "First, stop calling it 'the public space.' It's a theater lobby. Call it that. Now you can hope to create a different relationship with your community in that lobby, but stay clear about what it is."

p152

The User Experience *continued*

"Second, the central dynamic of your art form is the contract between actor and audience. Today, the contract says that I (the performer) will stand onstage and give you the show, and you (the audience) will sit quietly outside the proscenium and watch. So how can you take this basic contract and translate it into all the other things you are trying to make happen? Keep asking yourself 'Where is the proscenium?' Can the proscenium move out into the lobby? Could the lobby invite opportunities for performance, perhaps by your actors, or perhaps by audience members? Who knows? Can the Vera Katz Park invite performance? Can you create a virtual proscenium? Can you invert the relationship? Can the audience sometimes enter from the stage door instead of through the lobby?"

Our heads were spinning. And for a few weeks the team was stumped.

Then ideas began to surface about how we might create several strands of interaction: some of them permanent and technology-based; others temporary, low-tech and more event-based. I believe it was Patsy Freeman, the project manager from PFF, who said, "Well if we're going to take Ed at his word, why not hire a theatrical set and lighting designer to imagine the lobby as a set that can transform over and over again." And with that, we brought Nancy Keystone, the director and scenic designer, and Peter Maradudin, the lighting designer, on board to begin detailing how this "evolving" lobby could translate into physical terms.

> ...the central dynamic of your art form is the contract between actor and audience. Today, the contract says that I (the performer) will stand onstage and give you the show, and you (the audience) will sit quietly outside the proscenium and watch. So how can you take this basic contract and translate it into all the other things you are trying to make happen? Keep asking yourself 'Where is the proscenium?' Can the proscenium move out into the lobby? Could the lobby invite opportunities for performance, perhaps by your actors, or perhaps by audience members? Who knows? Can the Vera Katz Park invite performance? Can you create a virtual proscenium?
> *Edwin Schlossberg.* Designer of interactive experiences

The User Experience *continued*

We also engaged the local firm Second Story Interactive Studios to develop the interactive media in the lobby. Second Story has won awards for multimedia installations in museums all over the world (including the Smithsonian), but had not yet had a major project in Portland. Together we decided that there should be discrete places where the public could a) learn more about Portland Center Stage; b) learn more about the building's history; c) learn about the sustainable design and historic preservation aspects of the project. They also devised a donor wall that would live and breathe into the future.

And as the reality of the plans began to coalesce and the construction advanced, more and more people, supporters and skeptics alike, began to see that the Armory was going to be a very interesting place in Portland.

IF YOU LISTEN CAREFULLY, YOU MIGHT HEAR THE ECHOES OF THE PAST, THE MUSTERING OF TROOPS FOR THE SPANISH-AMERICAN WAR, BIG- TIME WRESTLING, BOXING, ROLLER DERBY, EVEN A PRESIDENTIAL ADDRESS! WHO COULD HAVE IMAGINED WHAT THIS BUILDING HAS EVOLVED INTO TODAY?

J. Greg Ness. Chairman of the Board,
Portland Center Stage

THE GERDING CAMPFIRE

On December 7, 2005, about 600 people gathered in the grand ballroom at the Governor Hotel for a special evening. For Bob and Diana Gerding, it was to be a Christmas Party for the Gerding/Edlen — Portland Center Stage family. For all of the guests, who had miraculously managed to keep the secret under wraps, the evening was designed to honor the Gerdings themselves.

It was no secret to anyone at PCS, or anyone involved with the Armory Project, that neither the theater's success, nor the Armory's realization would have been possible without the generosity, inexhaustible dedication, and real creativity of Bob and Diana. Bob had served on the Board of Directors for ten years now, and had seen the theater through every high and low imaginable. Now this funny, eccentric building, devised to protect the Chinese immigrant population in this budding Northwestern town from the threat of attack by a wary citizenry — a building that had hosted all manner of people and creatures, would soon be housing a different, or not so different breed of animal: actors.

And this funny building that so very many stories had been played out in, would become a home in which to share the stories of our community. The "campfire," — as Bob loved to call it, around which we would gather to find each other.

The building that had been constructed to "keep people out" would be in the business of "welcoming people in." And what better expression of this transformation than to see its name become: The Gerding Theater at the Armory.

DESIGNS FOR LIVING

Felt Hat Defines the Armory Experience

THE
FELT HAT

Our task was to help transform the Portland Armory from an old stone building into an inspiring new experience. We gathered a team of three designers, two architects, a cultural anthropologist and a writer to design new ways for people to build a relationship with the Armory. • How do you design an experience? The experience of a place is built incrementally, one intimate detail upon the next. First you talk to people. • We conducted several public forums, small group discussions and an online quantitative survey to determine what people want to experience in the spaces and venues that help make up the urban experience in Portland. Our research told us that people desire the following qualities: interactive space; different cultures and activities in one place; food venues; outdoor and indoor experiences; a hub of hubs and sustainability — environmental, economic, social. • Portlanders value integrity in projects. They also value quality and inspiration in design. They appreciate the beauty and accessibility of the outdoors and want to know that it will be respected and sustained. • Portlanders want things that are characteristic of the city and its own distinct culture. They do not want things that are slavishly copied from other places. In other words, they want no borrowed values. If something makes sense and has meaning, then Portlanders will invite it here. They are suspicious of growth for its own sake because they want things that will stand the test of time. Portlanders are more interested in quality than quantity. • When it comes to buildings and spaces, the people of Portland want to be inspired. Inspiration does not always come from large-scale spaces. It comes from spaces that are thoughtful, innovative, interesting, inviting, and sincerely express cultural, historical, functional and environmental values. They want spaces that are inclusive, accessible and welcoming. • Then you integrate the community's needs and the space's intrinsic values to create a design mandate: The Portland Armory inspires the anticipation of discovery. The Armory is a place where stories will be shared with a standing invitation for anyone to get to know them. The stories are about Portland theater, history, sustainability and community. The experience of the Armory is the anticipation of discovering the next story. As designers, as storytellers, it is our responsibility to inspire that anticipation. • Finally, you create formal design elements to build an experience that surprises, educates, stirs, challenges and delights. You develop programming that invites all manner of people to do many different kinds of things at different times of day in a single place. This guarantees that the space is in fact public — bright and alive at all hours. • Every brand is a kind of promise. It has no value until the promise is kept. A brand keeps its value by keeping its promise again and again. • The Armory is a promise. It's up to all of us to keep that promise.

The Felt Hat Experience Design Team was made up of The Felt Hat, a Portland design firm, in collaboration with Thom Walters, Stuart Emmons, Randy Higgins and Jake Murray.

SOLID MASS AND AIR

Theater in the Raw

ARMORY VOICES:
Design

**NANCY KEYSTONE
AND
PETER MARADUDIN**

The wonderful thing about the Armory and our assignment "to create a theatrical space" inside its lobby is that the building is already brilliantly theatrical and innately compelling. It's the kind of space we are both naturally drawn to, that gets our juices flowing — the raw materials, the scale, the shapes and how they reveal themselves, the textures, patinas, and grit, marked by many different human uses over time. It's a thrilling building, and a thrilling prospect to participate in creating a new space in which people will gather in the 21st century. • The building was stunning to begin with. In its pre-renovation form, it was: dirt floor; cavernous, sweeping overhead trusses; old brick, stone and mortar; outside turrets and towers; arched entrances; mysterious apertures — gun ports; windows; and who knows what — a combination of solid mass and air. We wanted to maintain the connection to and augment these very theatrical and sensuous elements for the new incarnation of the building. Essentially, we didn't want to ruin a great thing. • In looking at other buildings that inspire us, we found that a large percentage of them were sacred spaces — the Hagia Sophia in Istanbul, Matisse's Venice Chapel — or former industrial spaces that had been transformed for new uses in art or culture. There is a sense of holiness and meditation about these spaces, and a rough and elemental quality to their materials and geometries. We were drawn to the ways light functions — glowing votives and pendant fixtures. We felt that the Armory, though it had never been used in this way, had some of the qualities of these sacred spaces, and we wanted to emphasize these features. • We aimed to create a space that acts as a transition from the everyday world to the world of art. Everything in the lobby spaces should help support people's active engagement in the imminent theatrical event — to shift the focus, the brain waves, even the breath and heartbeat, in preparation for being part of the audience for a live performance. • By the time we were brought into the project, the building — including most of what's in the lobby spaces — was already designed. We concentrated on adding specific features and offered a variety of layouts for the different levels. We advocated for exposing more of the original Armory walls, more raw concrete, and mechanical elements (duct work, electrical hardware, etc.) in as many places as possible. Drawing on the way light played on the elemental materials in the building, we devised a large-scale "chandelier" using all raw materials — bare light bulbs, sockets, electrical cord — which hang on an elliptical metal structure from the ceiling. • We wanted to help facilitate the needs of Portland Center Stage, and to implement ways in which the different community "stories" could be told in unique and interactive ways. We hoped to introduce features that would engage people in a dialogue with the building, with the theater, with the community and most important, with each other. • All loftiness aside, we want the space to be fun and alive and beautiful and thrilling; we hope that people will be excited about the building and want to spend time there.

Nancy Keystone is a Los Angeles-based theater director / designer / writer, and visual artist. She is the founder / Artistic Director of Critical Mass Performance Group, and has directed and designed several productions at Portland Center Stage, including her own adaptation of *Antigone*.

Peter Maradudin's firm, First Circle, handles both theater and architectural lighting design. He has designed numerous productions for Portland Center Stage, and more than 300 productions around the country.

RETROFITTING THE ARMORY

Creative Solutions and Perilous Feats

Pat Conrad is the
Project Superintendent
for Hoffman Construction on
The Portland Armory.

In a new building construction project on the scale of the Armory, one ordinarily builds the foundation first, then the internal structure, and whatever needs to be inside the walls is brought in by crane. When we began the Armory renovation, the roof and walls were already in place, so we had to be extremely creative in the ways we built this building. These are just a few examples: To create 55,000 square feet of programming in a 20,000 square foot footprint, we had to excavate about 22,000 cubic yards of material, extract it through the two 14'x14' doors, then establish a new foundation 30 feet below grade. To shore the 115-year-old walls during excavation, we bored 50 diagonal feet in all four directions and used augur-cast steel soldier piles cast in concrete as tie backs. Each pile carried a 180,000-pound load. • An early challenge was getting a 50-ton crane safely through the door and lowered down a 45-degree grade to the bottom of a hole 30 feet deep. We go out of our way to confirm our techniques on risky moves like this, so one Saturday morning we took an 80-ton crane and lifted the 50-ton crane at a 45 degree angle. It bal-

anced well, and we went ahead. We then lowered the 50-ton crane with a tandem of 15-ton, triple axle wreckers — ordinarily used to haul 18-wheelers. Their grills were about a foot from the windows across the street. Again, extra hours of testing ensured the result. • Now, normally you can build interior walls and lift them into place. Inside the Armory, we had carpenters stick-build 65' tall, wooden back forms and then shoot Shotcrete against them — a very innovative use of this material. We had guys in fall-protection gear putting up these forms and scaffolding for six months. The structures were impressive. • To reach modern seismic loads that would allow us to tie the historic structure to the new one, thereby leaving the historic walls exposed throughout the building, we had to spec a dozen structural beams that were 4 feet tall by 70 feet long, and about ten tons each. Sounds small, but with the roof already on, we had to thread them through an existing man-door at about the 50 yard line and then continue through blocked-out holes in two concrete walls. The distance between the Armory and the building across Northwest Davis Street is only 60 feet. We brought the beams up the street on an angle, tucked them through the aperture with literally an inch to spare, and put them on a flatcar trolley with a 40' track we'd built to transition the beams inside. Then the crane put them in place for the welders, who made showers of sparks that were 60 feet long. It was a thrilling day. • To anchor the foundations for the elevators, our subcontractors used a custom technology they developed from years of working on oil rigs: a huge drill powered by a straight-8 Chevy engine, carburetor and all. An auto mechanic tuned it up. • With this and other internal combustion machines inside the building, we used exhaust scrubbers, bio-diesel fuel and CO testers to maintain safe air quality. The bio-diesel worked great. • As we wrapped up the excavation, we parked two large excavators at the western door that reached in and scooped out the ramp through the door into dump trucks waiting on the street. It was very risky but again, we did our homework and the task was a success.

NOISES OFF, WHISPERS HEARD

Building Silence for Sound

TOBIN COOLEY

Tobin Cooley, P.E, President of Listen Acoustics, has been a leader in the acoustics and audio/video engineering industry for 14 years, working on complex presentation, education, and entertainment environments for Portland Center Stage, Nike, Intel Columbia Sportswear, Nautilus and Microsoft.

Stacking two performance spaces and a rehearsal room within an existing building shell is one of the greatest acoustical challenges an engineer can face. Our job was to design the sound dynamics of the former Armory being retrofitted into theater spaces by isolating them from outside noise, from each other, and to optimize the acoustics inside the theaters.   •   We began by measuring the vibration levels coming from outside. A bus, for example, generates about 80-85 decibels (dBA) at 10 feet and our target background noise level is 25 dBA. We then optimized the "building-within-a-building" strategy using an acoustical engineering standard software program, EASE. The 30" solid brick outer wall, then the lobby, and finally a specially designed 12" concrete theater wall with different material types and thicknesses reduced unwanted resonance and sound transfer, absorbing exterior vibration and sound.   •   Excavation costs were too high and the water table too shallow to provide a large physical separation between the interior spaces, while under-floor ventilation created implications for sound transfer. Therefore, effective acoustical separation was achieved between the studio and main theater through two concrete slabs from 12" – 3' thick with three floating layers of 5/8" sheetrock, spring isolators, acoustical batt insulation and caulking, along with intensive penetration details. The Armory's HVAC (Heating, Ventilation and Air Conditioning) equipment was designed to be nearly inaudible, and the floor of the rehearsal theater on top is a floating concrete slab over the main stage's concrete ceiling.   •   The acoustical signature of the main theater was designed through materials selection, and by curving, faceting, and orienting hard surfaces. Seats were designed so that whether empty or full, room acoustics are kept constant. We added a variable acoustics component, which allows for moving curtains to adjust the reverberant energy off the ceiling. Most important, we worked integrally with building team partners to optimize the acoustical environment in transmitting voices and music from the stage to the audience so that it is engaging, natural, full, and balanced at all seats.

NORTHWEST SIDE STORY:
There's a (New) Place for Us

THE MAGIC WAND It is September, 2006, and we're in the final weeks before the building opens. As I write, it is one day before rehearsals begin for *West Side Story*. Nineteen actors arrived from New York last night, and they'll join their five local counterparts to begin learning that amazing Bernstein score in the morning. And I can't quite make it real yet. In a month people are going to finally inhabit this building again and breathe life into a space that has been "theory" for so very long. It feels wonderfully surreal.

It is difficult to conceive of how great a distance we have traveled.

I love to stand on NW 10th Avenue and watch passersby stop, look up and try to read the original insignia on the building's face. Cleaning up the exterior has made it possible to read the detail, and people stop and form the words aloud, "National Guards."

From the greenroom that is carved from a turret on NW 11th Avenue and Davis Street — you can see where the concrete floor met the wall three years ago: but who knew that entire worlds would appear both above and below that slab? Twenty-seven feet below the street that carries the streetcar buzzing past, there now appears a studio theater that will open with *I am My Own Wife* in two months. Up near the rafters, which once seemed miles away, our IT guys are

Magic Wand *continued*

installing phone lines and computer cable in the administrative offices while staff is moving in.

Heated and cooled by water-filled beams, the offices have carpets of recycled old carpets and sound absorption materials of recycled pop bottles. The desks are among the trusses, a conference room overlooks the lobby, and skylights — 41 to be exact — are everywhere. The rehearsal space is right in the middle of it all. It's an evocative work environment — evocative of things both grand and humble, all resolutely human and distinctly Northwest: industry and workaday routines, an overt respect for the elements, history and our limited place in it, art — those soaring trusses — and what it does for us, and the curative cast of natural light.

I like to sit in the mainstage theater. Just sit there and drink in how much better the sightlines are between the beautiful panels of recycled Douglas Fir on the walls, and how much leg room you have. The scale of the proscenium opening feels perfect: big enough for *West Side Story* but not too big for

Magic Wand *continued*

Pillowman. And most importantly — the furnishings are handsome, but not too eager for attention. So once the show starts, the show will be the star.

I like to stand with my arms leaning against the mezzanine rail and imagine what it will be like to watch audiences move through the space. To walk through the offices and watch the lights automatically decide to turn on when I appear, as if by magic. In the lobby I run my hand over the arch that was reconstructed by hand over the doorway to the main entrance and turn around to view the grand staircase that swoops down from the mezzanine, and catch the authenticity of those original brick walls, juxtaposed against great sheets of glass against steel against old growth timber. It takes my breath away every time I walk into the space.

Second Story has set up interactive theater guides next to the box office — two 40" touch-screens with dedicated speakers that only the user can hear. Another high-definition touch screen features discussions from some of Portland's leading minds on historic preservation and sustainable design. And there's another Second Story production — a huge "Historiscope" — an old-timey raree cabinet in the shape of the Armory that people can peep into to learn about the history of the building. All digital of course, but with a historic feel – entertaining and painlessly educational.

From the greenroom that is carved from a turret on NW 11th Avenue and Davis Street — you can see where the concrete floor met the wall three years ago: but who knew that entire worlds would appear both above and below that slab? Twenty-seven feet below the street that carries the streetcar buzzing past, there now appears a studio theater that will open with *I am My Own Wife* in two months.

Chris Coleman

p166

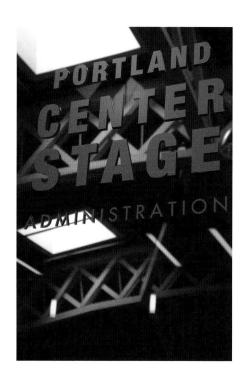

Magic Wand *continued*

You can't help but look up. The elliptical mezzanine aperture frames the view of the glorious trusses and gives you a sweeping vantage point of the building from the floor to the ceiling. The donor wall will be installed on the mezzanine in the next few days — a light sculpture that projects donors' names on glass through a software algorithm.

Not too long from now the firewall — a 25' tall sculpture of 70 hand-cast, amber-colored illumintaed, bullseye glass squares will be installed. Created by John Tess — the same guy who helped us get the historic tax credits for the building — the massive wall will glow like votive candles in a big cathedral. A huge, three-tiered chandelier, designed by Nancy Keystone and Peter Maradudin, is being installed in the next weeks like a star field above the floor. The Sliver Park — recently named Vera Katz Park — alongside Davis Street will be completed in December, green in the old and new sense. The trusses are lit, the Todd Oldham chairs arrive any day and the marquee is in place.

Magic Wand *continued*

I walk outside, turn the corner and look up. No pigeons in sight. OK, I lied. Two pigeons seem to have found a way to nestle into a little cubbyhole on the building's exterior that faces 10th Avenue. A sign? A blessing? A link, and a humble one at that, between past and future. This building has been a military training facility, a wrestling rink, an orchestra concert hall, a brewery and an empty, cavernous warehouse. It has hosted the First Regiment militia, track athletes, opera singers, presidents, circus animals, basketball teams, blues singers, wrestlers, skateboarders, sheepdogs, the jobless, championship tennis players, academy-award-winning actors, financiers and mayors.

For 115 years, the Armory has been many different things to many different people.

But to pigeons it's all the same.

It's all theater.

I'VE SPOKEN TO HUNDREDS OF PEOPLE ABOUT THIS PROJECT, AND IT RESONATES ON SO MANY LEVELS TO SO MANY DIFFERENT GROUPS. IN THE BEGINNING, I WAS SURPRISED BY THE INCREDIBLE ENERGY AND SUPPORT REFLECTED BACK AFTER TELLING OUR STORY. THEATER PEOPLE, PHILANTHROPISTS, BUSINESS PEOPLE, POLITICAL LEADERS, AND PEOPLE I MEET CASUALLY ALL WANT TO HEAR MORE. THOSE FROM NEW YORK, KANSAS CITY, LOS ANGELES, SEATTLE AND OTHER CITIES WANT TO KNOW HOW WE'VE DONE IT; THEY WANT TO DO THE SAME THING. AND WHEN I SHARE *THOSE* STORIES WITH THE PORTLAND COMMUNITY, PEOPLE HERE REALIZE HOW IMPORTANT IT IS TO SUPPORT THIS PROJECT. THIS WAS A GIFT TO OUR CITY THAT ALL SHOULD HAVE THE OPPORTUNITY TO BE PART OF AS FUNDERS, BENEFACTORS, AND ULTIMATELY ATTENDEES.
Julie Vigeland. Chair, Armory Theater Fund

OPENING WEEK

Tuesday, September 26, 2006: the first night I saw the public walk into the lobby of the Armory. I was standing on the balcony of the administrative offices leaning over the rail with (Patrick) Spike and Marty (Thompson) — our brilliant IT guys. The evening was an invited dress rehearsal for staff, volunteers and friends, and it was just so amazing to see the space begin to come to life as people walked in and gaped up at the chandelier (installed hours earlier) and the cleaned up trusses.

Wednesday evening we hosted the firms who built the building. I loved hearing from one steelworker who had built dozens of buildings in Portland but had never actually been invited back to see them in action. He wanted more tickets so he could bring his buddies back to see *West Side Story*.

Thursday mid-morning, Bob and I ran into each other in the lobby. It was our first time in the nearly completed building together. He hugged me, and neither of us could say much. I don't know that either of us knew if we would ever actually get to this moment. So we just stood there and soaked it in. It was an overwhelming experience to stand in a building in which each of us had invested so much of our hearts and souls, and to realize that it was going to surpass our imaginings.

Thursday mid-morning, Bob and I ran into each other in the lobby. It was our first time in the neary completed building together. I don't know that either of us knew if we would ever actually get to this moment. It was an overwhelming experience to stand in a building in which each of us had invested so much of our hearts and souls, and to realize that it was going to surpass our imaginings.

Chris Coleman

Opening Week *continued*

Saturday morning, *The Oregonian's* lead editorial ran with the headline: "Armory Renovation the City at its Best." It was an astonishing affirmation of the project's larger potential for impact and for the weaving of community, art, history and sustainability into one beautiful package.

Saturday evening, we closed off Couch Street behind Powell's Books and stretched long banquet tables out for the gala fundraising celebration. The tables were inspired by a photograph from a community celebration held in the Armory circa 1911. With an absolutely perfect September night holding rain at bay, it was hard to complain. Teddy Roosevelt (aka Keith McCough, looking terrific for a 150 year old) even showed up to offer the crowd an exhortation to action.

All 600 guests walked over to the building and had a chance to explore before we performed excerpts from the show. People were so honestly excited by the feel of the building, the combination of history and future represented, and by the warmth and sexiness of the

Opening Week *continued*

design. I think that perhaps the most gratifying comments came from Roger Cooke and Bob Van Brocklin, who had been PCS board members in the early days of the theater's life. Roger said: "Did you ever in your wildest dreams think that PCS would pull something like this off?" Bob said, "Not a chance. Not a chance in hell. But it's just so clear that this thing is going to succeed. It is amazing."

And then on Sunday we invited the community down for a big block party, with musical performances on an outdoor stage and booths lining Davis Street. We offered ticketed tours through the building and were sold out by 3:00 pm. Visitors were focused on the building's design and interactive "toys." (I noticed one father try to distract his nine-year-old son from the "Historiscope." Every time he pulled him away, the boy got back in line again.) By the end of the day, we had shown 5,000 people through the new building and the box office had done $35,000 of business ($10,000 is a banner day for Center Stage). By opening night, *West Side Story* had officially sold more tickets than any show in the theater's history.

... ON SUNDAY WE INVITED THE COMMUNITY DOWN FOR A BIG BLOCK PARTY. WE OFFERED TICKETED TOURS THROUGH THE BUILDING AND WERE SOLD OUT BY 3 PM. BY THE END OF THE DAY, WE HAD SHOWN 5,000 PEOPLE THROUGH THE NEW BUILDING AND THE BOX OFFICE HAD DONE $35,000 OF BUSINESS... BY OPENING NIGHT, *WEST SIDE STORY* HAD OFFICIALLY SOLD MORE TICKETS THAN ANY SHOW IN THE THEATER'S HISTORY.

Chris Coleman

Opening Week *continued*

Friday, October 6, 2006: Opening Night. After a week and a half of previews, you'd think that I would have relaxed, but I was still wired for sound. The combination of exhaustion and excitement had sent my obsessive-compulsive tendencies into high gear.

For me the evening began with a dinner in the newly inaugurated "Julie Vigeland Rehearsal Hall," with about 90 patrons. Jessica Andrews, Executive Director of Arizona Theatre Company, had flown in, as had Susie Medak, Managing Director at Berkeley Rep.

At the top of the show I was nervous because the actors were so ramped up for the first Jet/Shark scene. The show had already found a strong running energy, and if it started out too "amped" it could get out of control. But things quickly settled when Maria (played by Carey Brown) and Anita (played by Ivette Sosa), came on.

After a week and a half of battling with the balance of sound in the space, we had finally reached a quality of production that I was pleased with. (Though, I admit that my toes still clinched when the trombone dragged his cue in the middle of the prologue.)

I sat next to John Armour, our fight director, and his five-year-old son, Jack. Jack helped. He somehow allowed me to just take a breath, kick back and smile. I mean, what other option does the director have at that point? You might as well let go because there is no longer anything you can do.

And the performance, I had to admit, was pretty damn good. I even found myself touched at the end when the Jets first begin to pick up Tony's slain body. A lot of wet eyes in the house and a vigorous standing ovation.

Opening Week *continued*

Afterward, I felt like I was swimming in a sea of excitement and warm feedback. I was touched by comments from colleagues in the arts community, who seemed to see the Armory's success as a signal of larger things to come for all of us.

At the party afterward, people just hung out, chatted and danced. Rose Riordan (PCS associate artistic director), stopped by my office and we stood on the balcony and watched for several minutes. Just drinking it in. Gratified that people seemed to want to hang out in the space. Five little girls made up their own dance on the mezzanine level, and the revelry didn't seem ready to diminish when I dragged my tired self out of the building around midnight.

It was a thrilling ending (or beginning) to the Armory story. We had hoped and prayed and dreamed that the transformation of the building would create a warmer, more interactive, more human relationship with our community. In its first week of life, it was looking like that dream was going to come true.

In an interview that afternoon, the theater critic from *The Seattle Times* had described the space as feeling, "Portland Earthy Chic." In my curtain speech on opening night, I said that all day the thought in my head had been, "This is what Portland can do." The truly unique amalgam of energies and aspirations of the Armory would likely not have come together in quite the same way in any other city in the world. That I have had the enormous privilege to see this dream realized in a city I love so much is a great testament to the many, many people here who care about theater, about sustainability, about our history, and most clearly about making our community a more interesting place to live.

THE TRULY UNIQUE AMALGAM OF ENERGIES AND ASPIRATIONS OF THE ARMORY WOULD LIKELY NOT HAVE COME TOGETHER IN QUITE THE SAME WAY IN ANY OTHER CITY IN THE WORLD. THAT I HAVE HAD THE ENORMOUS PRIVILEGE TO SEE THIS DREAM REALIZED IN A CITY I LOVE SO MUCH, IS A GREAT TESTAMENT TO THE MANY, MANY PEOPLE HERE WHO CARE ABOUT THEATER, ABOUT SUSTAINABILITY, ABOUT OUR HISTORY, AND MOST CLEARLY ABOUT MAKING OUR COMMUNITY A MORE INTERESTING PLACE TO LIVE.

Chris Coleman

AN OPEN DOOR

Honoring Past Lives

ARMORY VOICES:
Community

JULIE METCALF KINNEY

Julie Metcalf Kinney is a
long-time community activist
who served as Board Chair and
then Executive Director for the
Native American Community
Development Corporation
LIHNAPO (Low Income
Housing for Native Americans
in Portland, Oregon). She was
on PDC's Urban Renewal
Advisory Committee for the
Interstate Max line and the
Advisory Committee for
the Portland Armory.

I've devoted many years to serving Native American and low-income communities, making sure the voices of color and/or the poor are remembered in venues they do not frequent. I feel I can speak with certainty about the emotional power and sense of pride people have for their neighborhoods — the older buildings, the streets and parks our families have enjoyed for generations. • For me, being born at Good Samaritan Hospital (in the newly added Wilcox Maternity Unit) and then twenty years later giving birth to my first child at the same hospital are especially important events that tie me to this neighborhood. Both births were performed by the same doctor — Dr. Elizabeth French — in the same Wilcox Unit. • The Armory is another resonant symbol; as a child, I remember passing the building many times when going to see my grandmother — who like many elders on limited income lived in the low-rent, old hotels. Northwest Portland was one of the most affordable areas for those in need, particularly the elderly. • At the age of 15, I began my working life living in a series of those affordable hotels and apartments close to my jobs. When walking downtown I passed the Armory many times. Others have reminisced about the Armory, telling me it was just about the only place in town that could hold large events indoors. In the early years the Armory was one of the only places people of color and younger crowds could attend concerts or cultural events. • My best friend recounts memories of her brother, Willard 'Battling' Nelson (aka Harold Penland), whom she remembers was the first local Native American boxer. The light-weight boxed a few times at the Armory between 1955 to 1959. My father spoke proudly about watching and meeting this young boxer. • Progress is always good for a thriving city; so is recognition of all the different kinds of people who live here now and those who came before us. The Pearl District is an entirely different neighborhood than it used to be. This change has been rapid and to some, scary. Honoring the history of a new cultural center restores balance. The new Armory is a place where *the doors will be open* for everybody for years to come. This simple statement is a most generous gesture to honor our people and those who have walked before us. I believe there are many spirits who are pleased to know the Armory building will be preserved and that it will be a space for the community to gather and enjoy the memories of days gone by as well as a place where new memories can be made.

THE NEW IN THE OLD

A Portland Landmark is Reborn

ARMORY VOICES:
Design

BRIAN
LIBBY

It used to be that historic and contemporary architecture were mutually exclusive. Sometimes we preserved old structures, with their enduring forms and memories of place. Where would London be without Westminster Abbey, or Egypt without the Pyramids? Other times architecture has sought new design frontiers with cutting-edge materials and methods, from the sleek midcentury modernism of Mies Van Der Rohe and Richard Neutra to today's revolution in sustainability. • The Gerding Theater at the Armory represents a third way, where old and new have come together to make a building that respects the past but lives for the future. • Visit the former Portland Armory today and you'll find this massive edifice of brick and wood is looking better than it has in more than a century. From the structural integrity of its soaring ceiling rafters to the freshly sandblasted façade, what was once a decaying old shell of its younger days is now a landmark reborn. • At the same time, although great attention has been paid to restoring the integrity of its original construction, the objective was not to make a new Armory. Rather, the Gerding Theater is a performance space and a cultural gathering place. And in so doing, the architects have nestled a striking example of contemporary architecture inside its historic envelope. There are two distinct portions of the Armory, even as they fit together like a hand in a glove. • This hybrid of old and new is also indicative of our time. Think of architect Sir Norman Foster's glass canopy over the Great Court at London's British Museum and his Hearst Building in Manhattan. Or the new Moynihan Station planned for New York City, with the old James Farley Post Office transformed into a new train station by the firms Skidmore Owings Merrill and Hellmuth, Obata + Kassabaum. In both cases, historic architecture is the foundation from which a 21st century building rises, not deferentially, but with pride and harmony. The Gerding Theater is no different. Or maybe it is, because this project also boasts the latest advances in sustainable design and construction, enough to earn a coveted LEED Platinum rating from the US Green Building Council. • And while it will make an ideal home for Portland Center Stage's many theatrical productions, the Gerding Theater also represents new thinking in arts facilities by acting as a cultural beacon even when the curtain is down. From its delightful Vera Katz Park to the multi-story lobby, the Gerding Theater at the Armory is a place where people can congregate day and night. The facility opens to and connects with its community not just as a theater but also as a place to hang out. Much as we can take pride in this stately historic local landmark, we can also come to know it as a familiar friend.

Brian Libby is a freelance writer and photographer living in Portland. He has previously written for the *New York Times*, *The Oregonian*, the *Christian Science Monitor*, among numerous publications.

BOOTS AND THE CITY

A Portland Armory Play Date

VICTORIA
BLAKE

Victoria Blake is a
fiction writer and book editor for
M Press/DH Press,
the prose division of
Dark Horse Comics.

I have a friend who wore cowboy boots to the theater.

· The friend is a poet, this was in New York, and he did it to pick up women. It was part of his look, along with the flowing, wide-collar white shirt, the tight jeans, and the pleasingly unruly hair. From his own account of this stage in his life, it worked.

· I asked him to take me to the theater one time, so I could see him in action.

· "It's more than the boots," he warned in the taxi heading downtown.

· "Really?"

· "Sure. Boots are nothing. Boots are boots," he said, picking up one booted foot and wiggling it in the air. The boots were beautiful, grey and black reptile skin of some sort, purchased on one of his poetic trips to South America.

· "Go on," I said, curious.

· "It's knowing the place," he replied. "It's having a plan."

· The taxi pulled up outside the theater, which advertised the play we were to see on a long, flapping marquee outside. It was still light, the blue, white light of summer, and I was sweating through the arm pits of my inconspicuous shirt.

· My friend, I noticed as he raised his arm to point across the street, wasn't sweating. That was part of the look, too. Calm and collected. A poet with a plan.

· "See that door?" he asked.

· I nodded.

· "Post-theater drinks," he said, obviously pleased with himself. "The lighting is fantastic. Then, if she's hungry, over there." His arm swung around, as if it were a crane, and pointed to another door down the block. I squinted, then nodded, unsure of where, exactly, he was pointing.

· He went on, explaining that the boots worked to catch a woman's interest, but the important part — the cincher — was to know where to take the woman after the play let out. Success, in my friend's mind, was measured not in the agreement to travel back uptown, but in the first step out of the theater, the moment he could take the stranger's elbow and lead her confidently down the block to a place he knew well, to a place he had taken other women before. Places have their own magic, he told me. It's just a matter of knowing where to go.

· That night, I hovered at a safe distance, pretending to read my Playbill, and watched as he scanned the milling crowd. When, after the event was through, he walked outside, I followed. I put my hand on his elbow and led him down the block.

"Another play," he said. "Another time."

This friend came to visit me a couple months ago, years after we had both left New York. I took him to our own downtown. As every Portlander does, I took him to see the Pearl where Powell's City of Books and Whole Foods are neighbors and gelato is just a stone's throw away.

· I pointed out the Armory building with a touch of pride.

· "The new home of Portland Center Stage," I bragged.

· "Really?" he asked, interested.

· "See that door," I said, pointing down the block. "Pre-theater pinot. See that, over there?" I asked, my arm swinging on its hinge. "Afterward, post-theater books."

· He smiled the charming, boyish smile of his, the one that used to work so well.

· "I brought my boots," he said.

A SLIVER OF PARADISE

Portland's Most Inviting Sidewalk

ARMORY VOICES:
Design

SCOTT MURASE

This passage is Murase's "blueprint" for the Armory's adjoining park, recently named the Vera Katz Park (previously referred to as Sliver Park). It describes both the materials and the concepts of his design.

Passage   Movement
Urban   People   Spaces   Gatherings
Conversations   Sounds   Surprise
Green

Expression of Landscape   Articulation

Materiality   Craft
Attention to Detail

Stone   Walls/Seating
Smooth   Chiseled   Carved
Light/Dark   Wet/Dry

Water   Source

Stormwater
Flow   Fall   Sounds
Channels

Celebrations!

Scott Murase is Principal of Murase Associates, which provides landscape architecture, urban design and public art services to a wide variety of public and private clients. With studios in Portland and Seattle, the firm has designed many projects that have contributed to the Pacific Northwest's spirit of place, gaining a reputation for creating high-quality designs that are sensitive to detail and material use, appropriate to place, and striking in visual form.

12 TOURS THE ARMORY

A One-Act Play on Design

Wieden+Kennedy 12
is an experiment
disguised as an advertising
school housed in the
Wieden +Kennedy
headquarters in
Portland, Oregon, USA.

CALEB
People were jealous when I told
them about our tour.

TIM
I miss being onstage.

JELLY
Sustainable building design looks
a lot harder than advertising.

JEREMY
I'd like to meet the person who
tightened the bolts on those
wooden trusses.

KELLY
Portland is a very thoughtful city.

SASHA
I hope James Brown gets down
here again.

PHILIP
I used to peek in the windows.

KATIE
It's precise/messy,
complicated/simple.

PATRICK
I'm not into hippies, but sustainable
architecture is cool.

LOREN
I want to flush a recycled
rainwater toilet.

JOE
"Sliver" Park? Come on.

ELISA
I wonder what it will smell like.

FUNDING SOURCES:

Mapping the Armory Revenue Streams

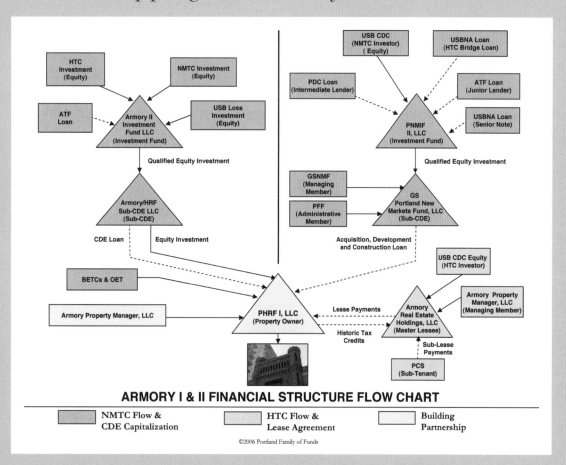

ARMORY I & II FINANCIAL STRUCTURE FLOW CHART

NMTC Flow &
CDE Capitalization

HTC Flow &
Lease Agreement

Building
Partnership

©2006 Portland Family of Funds

The Gerding Theater at the Armory was one of the first New Markets Tax Credits (NMTC) projects in the United States to utilize a leveraged financing structure, enabled by IRS ruling 2003-20, 2003-7 I.R.B. 465 of 2002. The initial transaction, which closed in April, 2004, included tax credits from GS New Markets Fund, 20% Historic Tax Credits, NMTC equity investment, and a loan by the Portland Development Commission. A second infusion of capital was achieved in December, 2005 in response to community desires for the lobby space and the highest levels of sustainable design, through tax credits from Historic Rehabilitation Fund, Oregon Business Energy Tax Credits, and tax credit equity investment.

VOICES OF THE ARMORY
SPONSORS

platinum

PORTLAND FAMILY OF FUNDS HOLDINGS, INC.
UNITED FUND ADVISORS
GERDING/EDLEN DEVELOPMENT
US BANK COMMUNITY
DEVELOPMENT CORPORATION

gold

GBD ARCHITECTS
GREEN BUILDING SERVICES
HERITAGE CONSULTING GROUP
MURASE ASSOCIATES
NIXON PEABODY LLP
NOVOGRADAC & COMPANY LLP

BIOGRAPHIES

CHRIS COLEMAN

Since joining Portland Center Stage as artistic director in May, 2000, Chris Coleman has directed *West Side Story, The Fantasticks, Celebrity Row, King Lear, Things of Dry Hours, Cat on a Hot Tin Roof, Batboy: The Musical, Man & Superman, Outrage, Much Ado About Nothing, The Seagull, Flesh and Blood, The Gimmick, A New Brain, A Christmas Carol* and *The Devils.* PCS produces eight plays each season plus its annual summer Playwrights' Festival, Just Add Water/West, and attracts an annual audience of more than 100,000. Before coming to Portland, Coleman was artistic director at Actor's Express in Atlanta and has directed at major theaters across the country. A native Atlantan, Chris holds a BFA from Baylor University and a MFA from Carnegie Mellon University.

KURT GOETZINGER

As the official photographer of the Armory renovation, Kurt Goetzinger is ideally suited to document the dramatic transformation of this historic building. His primary creative objective is to capture the essence of urban environments — often through architecture. A career in photography grew out of the thrill of traveling and the desire to capture and preserve ancient structures and cultures he found abroad. He has taken hundreds of photographs of the Armory since 2004. His Armory work was featured in a show at the Heathman Hotel, curated by the Elizabeth Leach Gallery and was also included in the October, 2006 issue of *Portland Monthly* in a photo essay designed by Pete Ivey.

BART KING

Bart King is the author of *An Architectural Guidebook to Portland,* which he claims is equally useful as both a doorstop and a cure for insomnia. Bart has also written the national bestseller *The Big Book of Boy Stuff* and (despite a gender disability) *The Big Book of Girl Stuff.* Bart acknowledges these people for their assistance in researching the Armory timeline: Bob Kingston, Donald R. Nelson, Kate Walker, Craig A. Mendenhall, Christopher Smith and Tim DuRoche.

CHRISTOPHER SMITH

Christopher Smith is Communications Manager for Portland Family of Funds, Managing Editor of *Voices of the Armory,* and a very amateur photographer who burned countless early-morning hours in the attempt to capture the few worthwhile frames the designer has generously included in this book.

PHOTO
CREDITS

Kurt Goetzinger: Cover, 16, 19, 21L, 25L+R, 27, 28T, 30L+M, 34, 37, 41T, 44T+B, 53, 55, 56L+R, 57, 58, 60, 61L, 63, 70L+R, 98, 106, 111, 112, 113, 115, 116L+R, 117, 118, 120, 121L&R, 122, 131, 132, 133, 135, 136L+R, 138, 140, 141L+R, 142, 143, 144T+B, 145, 146L+R, 148, 149, 150L+M+R, 152T+B, 153, 155, 156, 158, 164, 165, 167, 172B, 173R, 175T+B, 176, 177, 178L+R, 183

Christopher Smith: 7, 13M, 15, 21M, 22, 24T+B, 25M, 28B, 29, 30R, 36, 40, 41B, 51, 52, 61R, 64T+B, 65, 66L+R, 68, 69, 72, 75, 79, 80, 81, 83, 84L+M+R, 85, 86, 88, 89L+M+R, 91, 92T+B, 93, 94L+R, 97, 100T+B, 101, 103L+R, 104, 105, 127, 136M, 137, 163, 168L+M+R, 172T, 173L+M, 181

Sherri Diteman: 17, 20, 21R, 33, 39L
Second Story Interactive Studios: 169, 170L+R
Dick Kirschbaum: 39R
Birdboy, Dreamstime.com: 5L
James Hearn, Dreamstime.com: 6L

Other imagery

City of Portland Archives: *8T+M+B, 9M+B, 10T+M+B, 11M+B, 12T+B*
Oregon State Archives: *11T, 12M*
Courtesy of Bart King: *9T, Historic Postcard*
Courtesy of Joe Kregal: *11B, James Brown Poster*
Courtesy of GBD Architects: *13T, Armory Renderings*
Courtesy of Sandstrom Design: *13B, West Side Story poster,*
Concept and Design: Sandstrom Design; Illustrator: Howell Golson

VOICES OF THE ARMORY

PUBLISHER
Friends of the Armory and
Portland Family of Funds Holdings, Inc.

MANAGING EDITOR
Christopher Smith

EDITOR
Megan McMorran

DESIGNER
Kaie Wellman

Voices of the Armory is a publication of:

Friends of the Armory
c/o Portland Family of
Funds Holdings, Inc.
34 NW First Avenue, Suite 100
Portland Oregon 97209
503.226.1370
www.friendsofthearmory.com

PRINTED IN SINGAPORE

ACKNOWLEDGEMENTS
For their essential contributions to *Voices of the Armory*, Friends of the Armory would like to offer our sincere appreciation to the Platinum, Gold and Silver corporate sponsors; the 59 text contributors who gave selflessly of their time and expertise; Kaie Wellman, designer without peer; Megan McMorran, iron-willed editor; Chris Coleman for his bountiful algorithm of spirit, storytelling and sense of humor; Kurt Goetzinger for being unique and brilliant; Sherri Diteman for setting the bar high; Bob Kingston for the relentless research that gleaned Roosevelt, Taft and Wilson and bumped Harding who was someplace else; Bart King for his love of Portland (and fun); Lynn King for her sharp eyes at the last minute; Portland Family of Funds founding board of directors for its vision and unfailing support including Carl Talton (current executive chair), Ed Jensen, Hank Ashforth, Keith Barnes, Molly Bordonaro, Les Fahey, Nancy Floyd, Mike Henderson, Don Mazziotti (ex-officio board member while executive director, Portland Development Commission), Ralph Shaw, and Bill Campbell (secretary); Portland Family of Funds staff including Norris Lozano, Reynold Roeder, Colin Rowan, Cam Turner, Chris Hasle, Vangi Kessler, Neal Sacon, Stephen Brooks, Mark Skalski, Catherine Marel, Michael Nelson, Monika Shankar, Yupin Sinit, Patsy Feeman, Carrie Hoops, Stephen Scates, Patricia Easley and Christopher Smith; Friends of the Armory board including Thom Walters, Stephen Brooks, Jonathan Harms and Norris Lozano; the original Armory community advisory board including Sheila Holden (chair), Dick Cooley (vice-chair), Pauline Bradford, Sam Brooks, Gun Denhart, Bill Findlay, Tom Kelly, Julie Metcalf Kinney, Jennie Portis, Rick Saito, Duke Shepard, Greg Wolf and Ernest Warren; the board and staff of the Portland Development Commission; Portland Center Stage board of directors including J. Greg Ness (chair), Donna R. Huntsman, Robert K. (Bob) Gerding, Linda Wright, Douglas Smith, Jim Kean, Barbara West, Julie S. Vigeland, Christopher Babler, Kimberley A. Benson, Ellyn Bye, Paul DeBoni, Carol Dillin, Mark Edlen, Steve English, Robert L. Goodman, Tanner Halton, Jessica T. Hamilton, John C. Jay, Marilyn N. Jensen, Raymond N. Johnson, Nelson L. Jones, Marge Kafoury, Danielle Killpack, David Lezak, Ph.D., Schuyler Lininger, Jr. DC, Richard M. Linn, Alex Miller, Judy C. North, Michael V. Paul, Chris R. Rasmussen, Lawrence Rosencrantz, Mark Schlesinger, Howard Shapiro, Michael L. Smith, Tiffany Switzer, Lucy Tanner, E. Walter Van Valkenburg, Tim Wallace and Barbara Zappas; Portland Center Stage staff, especially Tim DuRoche for proving James Brown played here, and including Edith H. Love, Lisa "Smitty" Sanman, Kathy Budas, Thom Trick, Jenn Marantic, Rhianna Peterson, Frankie Binder, Kathryne Ewing, Creon Thorne, Robyn Hodges, Rose Riordan, Dawn Young, Megan Ward, Mead Hunter, Kelsey Tyler, Tom Haygood, Robert Welsh, Jeff Marchant, Geno Franco, Drew Dannhorn, Jeff Cone, Don Crossley, Casi Pacilio, Jeff Simmons, Mark Tynan, Jamie Hill, Pamela Schmerer, Joe Visnic, Charles T. Frasier, Marlene Montooth, Kristan Seemel, Kavita Jhaveri, Jessy Friedt, Laurene Jennings, T. Scott Foxe, Mariane Zenker, Josh Oakhurst, Ruth Walkowski, Patrick Spike, Marty Thompson, Talan Harrison, Lisa Comer, Alan King, Rebecca Felch, Steve Brian, Kim Berstler, Alanna Degner, Henry Diaz, Brian Durdick, Kali Eichner, Julia Golden, Juliet Marks, Charles Bonds, Peter Chordas, Greg Curry,

Barbra Havrilak, Adam Hogan, Hannah McKunas, Rhiannon Rodriguez, Audrey Sackett, Jeff Skora, Neil Taylor, John Wagner, Leigh Ann Weidlich, Clara Weishahn, Jacob Fenston, Devin Zoller, Michael Ortolano, Chris Rousseau, Alisha Flaumenbaum, Paula Buchert, Pam Jett-Goodrich, Barbara Casement, Larissa Cranmer, Bonnie Henderson-Winnie, Teri Cobourn and Jamie Lynne Powell-Herbold; The Armory Theater Fund board including J. Greg Ness, Tom Imeson, Michael L. Smith, Robert Van Brocklin and Ben Whiteley; the Armory Theater Fund Capital Campaign Committee, including Julie Vigeland (chair), Bruce Carey, Susie Desmond, Julie Dixon, Bob Gerding, Robert Goodman, Barbara Mahoney, H. Pat Ritz, Nicole Vogel, Thom Walters, Ted Winnowski, with Norris Lozano, J. Greg Ness, Colin Rowan and Christopher Smith (ex-officio members); Joe Kregal for dancing to James Brown in '65 and stashing the poster; Craig Mendenhall and Dick Kirschbaum; Jelly Helm; Spike Selby; Kelli J. Fields; Chris Powers; Father Arthur Schoenfeldt; The Community Development Financial Institutions Fund; Ecotrust for enlightening Chris Coleman; Pat Conrad, Loyce Gilpin and Justin Patterson; Elaine Aye and Alan Scott; Dana Plautz; Alex Ruiz; Amie Abbott; Judy Tuttle; Jesse Beason; Scott Poole; and our friends and families for their patience during our long days and nights working on this supremely satisfying project.

ABOUT FRIENDS OF THE ARMORY
The mission of Friends of the Armory is to serve as a collaborative resource that connects theater and the arts to the broader community through the catalytic power of sustainable urban development.

The purposes of the Friends of the Armory, as set forth in its Articles of Organization, are:

1. To promote the arts through creative use of the Armory Building's "community space," (main lobby, mezzanine, studio theater lobby) and supporting arts and theater groups that qualify as Section 501(c)(3) organizations, in their use of and improvements to the Portland Armory.

2. To provide education regarding green building practices by organizing and sponsoring educational events, exhibits and other activities, including education regarding green building practices used in the restoration of the Portland Armory, and by facilitating improvements to the Portland Armory that further environmentally sustainable building practices.

3. To foster greater community appreciation of the historic Portland Armory by organizing and sponsoring events, exhibits and other activities educating the community about the building and its roll in the history of the community.

NET PROCEEDS FROM THE SALE OF *VOICES* BENEFIT FRIENDS OF THE ARMORY, A NONPROFIT ORGANIZATION